NO REDEMPTION IN THE REARVIEW MIRROR

*A 90-Day Journey Intended to Help You Navigate Change
and Reach Your Divine Destination*

SHARON PIZZO

Trilogy Christian Publishers
A Wholly Owned Subsidiary of Trinity Broadcasting Network
2442 Michelle Drive
Tustin, CA 92780

For information, address Trilogy Christian Publishing
Rights Department, 2442 Michelle Drive, Tustin, Ca 92780.
Trilogy Christian Publishing/ TBN and colophon are trademarks of Trinity Broadcasting Network.

For information about special discounts for bulk purchases, please contact Trilogy Christian Publishing.

Manufactured in the United States of America

Trilogy Disclaimer: The views and content expressed in this book are those of the author and may not necessarily reflect the views and doctrine of Trilogy Christian Publishing or the Trinity Broadcasting Network.

10 9 8 7 6 5 4 3 2 1

Library of Congress Cataloging-in-Publication Data is available.

ISBN 978-1-64773-905-8 (Print Book)
ISBN 978-1-64773-906-5 (ebook)

DEDICATION

*T*his book is dedicated to my Lord and Savior, who pulled me from the miry pit and placed my feet upon the Rock of Christ! The Holy Spirit was my guided hand, while Jesus accompanied me as I typed this inspired devotional to prayerfully share with others stalled by life's choices, decisions, past fears, and disappointing outcomes. I pray you receive, with each turned page, a newfound promised hope of His everlasting grace, along with the knowledge of His blessed plan for your future.

To Karl, my husband and best friend, who believed in me when I didn't believe in myself, and who supported this endeavor as my armor bearer who girds me in prayer. He is, and remains to be, the wind beneath my wings and the love of my life forevermore!

And to Nicholas, Daniel, Vincent, and David, because you are all my "whys"! Love you all!

INTRODUCTION

*H*ave you taken to the road often enough that you begin to take notice of very specific items in your vehicle that perhaps you never noticed before? I have been that person of remarkable intent. On an excursion one afternoon, I took pause to realize that my "rearview mirror" reflected all those cars that either trailed too close or were very far behind. The ones that seem to shadow my space increased my anxiety as they seemed to kiss my bumper as an uninvited guest. The vehicles in the distance appeared to be minute in comparison and innocuous in nature. Yet my car's windshield, which I steadily gazed upon, enabled me to clearly navigate my journey—which was expansive and full of possibilities. I was able to move in a forward direction toward a new destination without fearing what was behind me, as long as I continued in my lane of grace.

How often does your past speak out to you as if you were a criminal on trial? How many times do you take steps forward in your faith walk only to have the enemy cause you to stumble backward? Perhaps these thoughts have resonated with your heart, mind, and spirit. Perhaps they speak louder than the voice of reason and truth because the negative has become more palatable than the positive. Life can be challenging, especially when strongholds capture your mind from a young age and bind the roots of self-deception throughout your adolescent years. We begin to appoint credence to the insidious lies from the past instead of to the truth of a newly transformed self. For me, these have been true realities during my new life of redemption in Jesus Christ. We all need to heal from past mistakes, damaging decisions, cruel adjectives, and lofty actions. Then why do we slide back to the past when Jesus promises that our transgressions have been forgiven once we repent of them? How can we begin to move ourselves forward with confidence undergirded by the finished work of Calvary's bloodstained cross?

Jesus tells us in Romans 12:2, *"Do not conform to the pattern of this world, but be transformed by the renewing of your mind. Then you will be able to test and approve what God's will is—his good, pleasing and perfect will."*

We are not called to configure ourselves back into the cookie cutters of our past lives and lies, but we are to be transformed by the shedding of the conformity of this worldly format.

This devotional was inspired by the title that the Lord placed upon my heart years ago. I actually began penning a book about my testimony that lay dormant in my computer file for some time. Each chapter I wrote was a painful purge to the Lord and a love letter written in gratitude for the gift of my salvation. I always found, for some unassuming reason, that while I was driving, the bizarre thoughts would penetrate my mind. Many were not of the Lord, so immediately I cast them aside. But how often they would creep back, obtrusively, and uninvited to haunt my day as an intruding spirit. Can I get a witness? But how often I desperately would call upon the name of Jesus, the Lover of my soul, to vanquish the thoughts and patterns from the past.

Historically, it takes thirty days to create a behavior habit, whether good or bad. According to the MayoClinic.org, wellness coach Amy Charland states that "it takes 30 days, which is the common timeframe for putting new habits into practice. It can take many times over for it to be a natural process."

We have to strive to persevere forward in order to run the race of endurance that is set before us. The awareness of the movement of our process can be accompanied by proficient journaling to discover our assets and liabilities.

> *And let us run with perseverance the race marked out for us, fixing our eyes on Jesus, the pioneer and perfecter of faith. For the joy set before him he endured the cross, scorning its shame, and sat down at the right hand of the throne of God.*
>
> —Hebrews 12:1–2 NIV

Beloved, as a fifth-career pastor, I have had much time to restart my race with Jesus. We were never created by the Master Potter with the motive to navigate this life's journey unescorted. I will never attain perfection within my broken self alone, but only through the atoning work of Christ's perfection that leads to a "perfected" faith.

My inspiration to pen this 90-day devotional is to spark change in your thoughts, actions, and behaviors to reflect Jesus Christ. To metamorphose into the image of the Holy One who originally designed you, and not the past that tried to redefine you.

The **first thirty days** are to establish your identity in Christ with relation to His overarching plan. It is so crucial to our Christian lifestyle that we die to our flesh-filled proclivities daily. As blood-bought believers, we need to cooperate with God's purpose for our lives so we can eagerly seize a **"known life"** in Jesus.

The **next thirty days** are designed to initially change a habit or create a new behavior grounded in Christ. Intentionally, we need to surrender those bondages and burdensome yokes to the foot of the cross to achieve a fully **"transformed life"** in Jesus.

The **final thirty days** are rooted in Scriptures that substantiate our ownership and accessibility to a life fully lived for Christ. We, as heirs to the throne and change agents of the Holy Spirit, can declare the hope for attaining a truly **"redeemed life"** in Jesus.

As you navigate through this devotional, I invite you to capture your accounts along the way. I have provided, for each day, a journal space for your thoughts; what you are learning about yourself; what is defining your crossroads for destination; what you need to leave behind; and how the new excursion will inspire transformation. So dear friend, grab your book, pack your Bible, and invite the Holy Spirit to copilot your journey forward, as there is *"no redemption in the rearview mirror"*!

FIRST 30 DAYS:
"A KNOWN
LIFE IN HIM"

DAY 1

"Write the vision and engrave it plainly on [clay] tablets so that the one who reads it will run. For the vision is yet for the appointed [future] time. It hurries toward the goal [of fulfilment]; it will not fail. Even though it delays, wait [patiently] for it, because it will certainly come; it will not delay."
—Habakkuk 2:2–3 AMP

~ ~ ~ ~ ~ ~ ~ ~ ~ ~

*T*here is a determined and specific time in the watchful eyes of the Lord. God knows His plan and the tapestry that will need to unfold in the midst of our lives as it weaves an agenda. In the time of waiting, we are called to study and proclaim the revelation while waiting for its fulfillment to come forth. But as we tarry, we are called to "pen the vision" for the plan that God has designed for us.

Everything in the economy of Christ comes in due season and at the perfect time. We, however, are required to be patient in the waiting room of our goals, dreams, and aspirations. In that time frame, we are instructed to write the "vision" down. Are you aware of the framework that the Lord has for provided for you? Are you in a season of waiting and watching, or preparing and praying? They all seem to work in tandem with one another as the masterpiece reveals itself to us day by day.

Perhaps there are things that need to be in order before you establish your future destination. What gets in your way? Do you get in your own way? You first need to till the soil before planting the seeds for the mighty harvest. Discern your strategies while beginning the process of uncovering the obstacles that are blocking your clarity. Ready yourself for when the Lord commissions you to advance as He alone directs your steps.

Action Step of Faith: Be aware for when your launching time will emerge. Document the genesis of your vision as obstacles begin to dissolve from your view.

~~~~~~~~~~~~~~~

Lord, I pray for a deeper revelation to follow Your ordained plan for my life. Help me to tarry with You to release my past or relinquish my present, in order that I can grasp with a confident conviction, a hope-filled future. Amen.

_____
_____
_____
_____
_____
_____
_____
_____
_____
_____
_____
_____
_____
_____
_____
_____
_____
_____
_____
_____
_____
_____
_____

*In their hearts humans plan their course, but
the LORD establishes their steps.*
—Proverbs 16:9 NIV

~~~~~~~~~~

W here does your determination stem from, and where does it lead you? God has created us with gifts and abilities unique only to ourselves. We are not to compare our gifts with another, but we are to utilize them to prosper in God's plan and purpose in our lives.

Joseph's plan that morning was not to end up thrown in a pit at the hands of his brothers! And it was not Daniel's plan to share a space with some ferocious lions! God had a destiny in mind for them both that would not be thwarted by man. Joseph's pit was a ticket to a palace address, and Daniel's was to be made a royal master instead of lunch. These were both part of the Master's plan!

Are you cooperating with God in this season of reimagining your plan? We need to seek God with our whole hearts to gain insight into His navigational program for our steps. If you can't see His plan clearly, it is time to identify the "mountain" blocking your view. Perhaps a season in the pit or even the lions' den can draw us closer to God as our total reliance depends on His direction. This is the time to learn to "lean not on our understanding," but to acknowledge Him to straighten and direct our path (see Proverbs 3:5–6 NIV). Before we can begin the journey forward, this may be the season of clearing the baggage that keeps you stuck in a "rut" thinking process.

Action Step of Faith: Today allow the Holy Spirit to lead you to the foot of the cross. Invite God to shine His light brightly for your ability to discern the boulder that blocks your route to success.

~~~~~~~~~~~~~~~

Lord, help me to see You instead of all my regrets, mistakes, and bad decisions that have led me astray and off course. Father, I pray to seek You at the altar of grace, where my forgiveness lies dormant waiting for me to find You in that space of grace. May this be the day of total surrender to completely pursue Your master plan that has been fashioned specifically for me. Amen.

_____
_____
_____
_____
_____
_____
_____
_____
_____
_____
_____
_____
_____
_____
_____
_____
_____
_____
_____
_____
_____
_____

DAY 3

See what great love the Father has lavished on
us, that we should be called the children of God!
And that is what we are!

—1 John 3:1 NIV

*D*o you know who you are and to whom you belong? You are a child of God, the Most-High Messiah, who calls you beloved! Now is the time to no longer be an outsider in your relationship with your Savior. Let this day mark your departure from being unsure to being truly confident in your heritage in the Kingdom of God. Allow yourself to be washed by the Word of the Lord to overflow and have the His truth immerse your soul. Step into the knowledge and depth of the love of your Creator to His adorned creation. If you don't have that relationship with Jesus, in this breath and moment, invite Him into your heart. Repent with a deep and genuine submission to receive His gift of forgiveness and salvation. Believe with a newfound trust, love with the love He offers you, and Jesus will prosper your mustard seed of faith as He waters the offering of your embrace to follow Him. Welcome, adopted child of God, into the Kingdom of glory.

Continue to deny yourself as you follow Jesus, pick up your cross, and lose your past life as you are newly born today! For those who are saved, perhaps today realign your sinner's prayer with a fresh declaration of identity in Christ as we are still citizens of this culture.

Action Step of Faith: Today, understand who you are in Christ by journaling what actions identify you as a child of God in your witness each day. Ask the Holy Spirit to clarify your daily holy habits.

~~~~~~~~~~~~~~

Lord, guide me on this journey to understand my identity in Christ. Prayerfully this day will endeavor a new road with endless possibilities, all leading to Your doorway. Gracious Father, help me to remain on this narrow road of life, and even as the tide pulls me astray, prayerfully I will always find my way back to You! Amen.

_____
_____
_____
_____
_____
_____
_____
_____
_____
_____
_____
_____
_____
_____
_____
_____
_____
_____
_____
_____
_____
_____

DAY 4

*"Then you will call on me and come and pray
to me, and I will listen to you. You will seek me
and find me when you seek me with all your
heart."*

—Jeremiah 29:12–13 NIV

*D*o you know the definition of being "wholehearted"? That is imparting love completely and without reservation. That is the love we experience from our Father God, and that is the response He awaits from us. Jesus waits in the secret place for us to come to Him and to pray when no one is watching (Matthew 6:6). This is done with a whole heart of desire to be with the Lord and to spend time in prayer.

When we seek God in this holy place, we find Him there waiting for us! Can you imagine—the God, the Creator of all things, waits for us! Yes, that is because He loves us and desires our time to be spent well with Him. In that space of grace, God reveals His plans, His will, and His nature to us in this intimate relationship. When we enter into our time alone with our Savior, it is with a pursuit of love that hungers after the tenets of our faith to blot out the wounds of this world. We bring to Him our adoration with blessing, our confession with sincerity, our thanksgiving with gratitude, and then our petitions of prayer.

How do you enter into your secret place with the Lord? Do you shut out all distractions, negative reactions, and worldly attractions so you can surrender yourself fully in that divine time of prayer? Submit fully so you won't miss a whisper from His breath into your inclined ear.

Action Step of Faith: Take your journal with you into your prayer time and record what the Spirit speaks to your soul! So often we think we will remember, but when we forget, sometimes it's a lost gem.

~~~~~~~~~~~~~~

Father God, I pray for a deep fervor to seek You with all my heart. Lord, let my busyness never usurp my time spent with You. Lord, insert a deep desire within my soul to seek You above all else, because I know I will find You waiting to embrace me, Your child. Amen.

_____
_____
_____
_____
_____
_____
_____
_____
_____
_____
_____
_____
_____
_____
_____
_____
_____
_____
_____
_____
_____

DAY
5

*"Seek the Kingdom of God above all else, and
live righteously, and he will give you everything
you need."*

—Matthew 6:33 NLT

~~~~~~~~~~~

*W*hen you first awake in the morning hours, what is your first thought? Who or what do you seek after in your firstfruits of the day? The One of whom we need to focus first should be the Holy One who awakens us each morning! Allow yourself to come into His presence first before checking your phone, brushing your teeth, or even leaving your bed. Remain in that quiet space of time before the day begins and the kids start clamoring for your attention. Ease into a meditative pause and seek God for all that you need that lies within the pulls and pushes of your day. Seek Him in your upright living and engage Jesus to lead you on the pathway forward.

When we seek His Kingdom before all others, we can relinquish the cries of the idols tugging for our momentary contemplations. Only when we tarry with God first, can we move into our day with an even flow of peace, joy, gentleness, goodness, kindness, self-control, patience, humility, and faithfulness (see Galatians 5:22–23). Therefore, with these ripened fruits can we remain in tandem with the righteousness that has been God-ordained.

Beloved, what is your acuity to remain focused in the morning hour? When you give God your time first, what does He provide to you in return? Does your initial morning offering of the day spent with the Lord enable a more productive atmosphere to acknowledge the Holy Spirit's work in your life?

Action Step of Faith: Begin to be more aware of your morning routine. Is God a part of your daily plan? Can you begin to infuse a morning prayer devotional into the start of your day? Journal the difference it begins to make in your faith walk and in the spiritual abundance of your fruit!

~ ~ ~ ~ ~ ~ ~ ~ ~ ~ ~ ~ ~ ~

Holy Spirit, provide to me the conviction to yield to that space of grace more than anything else to kickstart my day. I pray for a deeper revelation of Your agape love for me as You wait upon me in the elegance of simplicity in the break of dawn. Amen.

*Jesus replied to them. "I am the Bread of Life. The
one who comes to Me will never be hungry, and the
one who believes in Me, [as Savior] will never be
thirsty [for that one will be sustained spiritually]."*
—John 6:35 AMP

*I*n our lifetimes, we start and stop diets or healthy eating trends
to lose some weight, gain more energy, and attempt to feel
better from the inside out. How many times has that plan been
successful? What have been the sustainable challenges you've had
to reach your goal? For me, anything I attempt to accomplish in
my own strength and aptitude outside of the Holy Spirit's guidance usually fails. My plan without the leading of God is not sup-
portable as it lacks viability. In turn, when our plan fails, we often
feel deflated and defeated, which brings us back to the unwanted
dietary habits we are so desperately attempting to break.

Jesus reminds us that our relationship with Him requires
the characteristic of sustainability. Jesus is the enduring Savior,
whereby the believer will never hunger or thirst for anything that
will quench their faith. All that you ever need will be in constant
supply with an abundant increase in all things that are fortified by
the Lord. Jesus provides spiritual sustenance as He invites you to
His banquet table, which has been prepared on your behalf.

How often do you invite Jesus into the struggles of your life?
How often do you remember that He provided the Holy Ghost as a
personal cheerleader who wants you to attain your purpose-driven
goals? It is a good and godly endeavor to eat healthy since we
embody the Holy Spirit within our earthen temples. We are called
to honor God with our bodies, as we were bought with a price and
have been reconciled through Christ (1 Corinthians 6:19–20).

Action Step of Faith: Where do you get stuck? Begin a food journal to discover any patterns or sabotage "mindsets" that throw you off course in your goal of weight loss, a healthier dietary plan, or just learning to be patient with yourself. We are called to love one another, but that includes "yourself"! Don't loathe your body, but embrace the beautiful image that God fashioned when He created You!

~ ~ ~ ~ ~ ~ ~ ~ ~ ~ ~ ~ ~ ~

Jesus my Lord, today I invite You to guide my dietary plans for physical nutrition as You sustain my spiritual essence. Holy Spirit, convict me to stay on course and remember that my body is the temple that is inhabited by the Holy One. This is a new day for me to forget my past eating failures and allow myself the ability to move forward in new, healthier habits and to love myself through this process. Amen.

_____

_____

_____

_____

_____

_____

_____

_____

_____

_____

_____

_____

_____

_____

_____

_____

_____

_____

DAY 7

LORD himself goes before you and The will be with you; he will never leave you nor forsake you. Do not be afraid; do not be discouraged.
—Deuteronomy 31:8 NIV

~ ~ ~ ~ ~ ~ ~ ~ ~ ~

*H*ave you ever experienced not being able to locate your glasses? You know you just had them, and they couldn't have gone too far. You look for almost twenty minutes, searching everywhere, including the freezer, out of sheer desperation, also knowing there's no one home to witness that possible hiding place. Then you discover that your glasses have been propped masterfully on the top of your head! Truth be told, I have experienced that more than once in my recent past, just out of being too busy to be aware that they never left my "person." They were there, perched on my head, all along, as in my busyness I lost track of knowing they were present.

Sometimes our faith journey can feel the same way when we lose sight of Jesus, but He never leaves our side. He is always with us, even if we are not in step with Him! He is a forever, faithful friend for our life's journey! You never have to be fearful, but live your life "faith-filled," knowing that He dwells within you and remains closer than a brother or sister ever could! I love this word picture of God above us, Jesus next to us, and the Holy Spirt within us! We are covered from the inside out and all around by our Creator!

Even though you might have been lost, you are now found and known to your Redeemer! Call upon His name and be confident that He hears your voice! Even if you feel distant, He never moves away. Even if you feel out of touch, He always extends His mighty hand to yours. Even if you feel lost, you are held by His zealous embrace.

Action Step of Faith: Mediate on the truth that God loved you first and has counted every hair upon your head. Spend time in His presence when you feel distant and allow Him to saturate your spirit with His fervent love for you, His beloved child.

~~~~~~~~~~~~~~~

Loving Lord, let my breath only speak Your name as I sense Your presence ever so clearly. Help me to stay still long enough to have Your Spirit capture my heart when I feel lost, distant, or frightened. O Lord, I give myself to You as a sacrificial offering with all my love as I receive Your unending gift of grace, mercy, and peace. Amen.

DAY
8

*Then the Lord God formed [that is, created the
body of] man from the dust of the ground, and
breathed into his nostrils the breath of life; and
the man became a living being [an individual
complete in body and spirit].*

—Genesis 2:7 AMP

O ur Creator took time and effort fashioning His creation. He created us by designing our bodies out of mud and clay, as He transformed us into something new. God breathed His breath of life into us as He breathed the first fresh breath into Adam. God gives to us, His creation, a cleansing exhalation when we succumb from the polluted atmosphere of this world to His invitation of a "new life."

The breath of God is the initial indicator of our lungs filled with the miracle of life from on high. God created us to be in relationship with Him as a living being but also to house the Holy Spirit. God gave Adam, through the Edenic Covenant, dominion over all living things. In the plan of man, the Lord granted us a special place in His creation.

As He is the potter and we are the clay, He shapes us into an acceptable vessel so that we might be molded into our intended identification marked by His fingerprints (Jeremiah 18:4). Do you know that your breath of life is a gift from God? Each morning, receive a fresh breath for the new day ahead. God created you "on purpose" for a purpose as He continues to form you for that specific design.

Action Step of Faith: Spend time seeking God's purpose for your life. Be aware of your breath as you mediate on the Word. Breathe in the truth of your identity, promises, and calling in this season of your life. With each inhalation of breath, gain inspiration for your motivation. Breathe out any toxicity that is not of the Lord so that you may replenish the supply of His refreshing grace.

~~~~~~~~~~~~~~~

Majestic Creator, may I take in a deep breath of Your adoration and then expel anything that is not of You this day. Teach me to desire the tenets of heavenly realms over anything this world could offer. Lord, consume me completely as an earthen vessel so You can melt me, mold me, and fill me, only to use me. Amen.

_____
_____
_____
_____
_____
_____
_____
_____
_____
_____
_____
_____
_____
_____
_____
_____
_____
_____
_____
_____

Fixing our eyes on Jesus, the author and per-
fecter of faith, who for the joy set before Him
endured the cross, despising the shame, and has
sat down at the right hand of the throne of God.
For consider Him who has endured such hostil-
ity by sinners against Himself, so that you will
not grow weary and lose heart.
—Hebrews 12:2–3 NASB

*I*n order for a novelist to write a book, there must be that spark
of intention that leads to the telling of a story. Every book
has a beginning that invites us into the inspired purpose, then a
middle that reveals the plot, and the ending, which illuminates a
fully "understood" completion. The author's purpose is to share
the story with such conviction that it engages the reader to prevail to the final page. The Greek word for "author" used in this
verse when translated means "prince" or "captain." Christ not only
records our story, but He is the Captain who guides us and the
Prince who presides over our lives.

Jesus was present at your conception, and He will be there
to greet you at your entrance to heaven. Jesus, who is the Author
of your life, intercedes on your behalf for you to persevere unto its
completion. God hovers as He captures the years that pass in your
storybook of life. Our Savior gives us the ability to act out our personal dramas with "free will," but how much is ascertained in substantiating a genuine state of faith that will eternally play itself out?

The author of Hebrews is reminding us in this passage that
Jesus has done everything necessary for us to be steadfast in our belief.
His intention to endure on the cross was not esteemed in the agony
but the ecstasy of the crown. He wants us not to grow weary in the
valley seasons of life, but to be steadfast for the eternal rewards. How

do you continue to keep your eyes fixed on Jesus when life is turbulent and your original designation becomes out of sync? Remember to set your gaze upon the Holy One, who knitted you into existence, unto sanctification that is only found in Him. When we enter into places of hardship, we are co-heirs of Calvary's cross as His story is ours. He died so you can live with abundant joy. He suffered so you can abide victoriously. Allow Jesus to assist as the publisher of your life's manuscript as He desires to be the co-author of your story!

Action Step of Faith: Do you provide room for God to write your story, or do you always steal His pen? Today, what will you voluntarily surrender to God in order for Him to create revisions in your life's account? How will this change the narrative of your story?

~~~~~~~~~~~~~~

Lord Jesus, come and teach me to abide in You as you forever abide in me. I pray for an emboldened trust to unfold as together we chronicle my life hand in hand. May I always yield unto Your will. Amen.

_____
_____
_____
_____
_____
_____
_____
_____
_____
_____
_____
_____

"My sheep listen to my voice; I know them, and they follow me. I give them eternal life, and they shall never perish; not one will snatch them out of my hand."

—John 10:27–28 NIV

~ ~ ~ ~ ~ ~ ~ ~ ~ ~

*A*s a young child, my son and I were separated at a very crowded harvest festival. I recall turning around for one minute, and he was nowhere to be found. I believe my heart stopped for a moment, and everything that was swirling around me seemed to pause and fade away. All I could feel was a sick feeling overwhelming my body as I became desperately helpless. My only thought was to yell his name as loudly as I could over all the crowd. Then all of a sudden, there he was again in my sight because he could recognize my voice and navigate his way back to me. Thank the Lord that this story had a happy ending.

How many times has the Lord cried out to you? Perhaps you have been stricken with a deaf ear at that particular moment. Or you don't recognize His voice, since you have not been interfacing too much these days. Or have you gone astray for some time? Call upon the name of Jesus. He knows you, beloved, as He loved you first. His sheep are well-acquainted with His voice.

God creates us to enter into fellowship with Him no matter the divisive behaviors, damaging decisions, or major mistakes we have made in our lives. His desire is that we invite Him into our mess so a message can be born. It is through the most painful tests that our most victorious testimonies are discovered. But we need to listen for His voice because we are known by our Good Shepherd as we are instructed to follow Him. Even though the enemy will be underfoot, God has you protected with His mighty hand. Jesus sticks closer than a relative, and He will always be by your side. He will leave the ninety-nine others to gather you back to His fold.

Action Step of Faith: When you begin to incline left as opposed to right, call upon His name and listen for His voice. Be aware of your worldly positioning in situations that might find you lost. Invite the Holy Spirit to be your GPS, your God Positioning System, so you can always find your way back home.

~~~~~~~~~~~~~~~

Gracious, Loving Shepherd, keep me safe in Your green pastures and always hold me close to You. Help me incline to hear Your voice above all the others vying for my attention in this hour. O Lord, when I get turned around by the situations of this world, may I always be found by Your protective hand. Amen.

DAY 11

"But while they were on their way to buy the oil, the bridegroom arrived. The virgins who were ready went in with him to the wedding banquet. And the door was shut."

—Matthew 25:10 NIV

~~~~~~~~~~~

S ome of us wait all of our lives for the perfect mate. We prepare for a first date, then court for a while, and if all goes well, we hope for a possible marriage proposal. So many of us spend our lives dreaming of the day we can find that perfect person to share our lives, while others never meet "Mister or Miss Right." Or maybe you acquiesced into a wedding contract only to find yourself disunited and separated from your mate. With Jesus in your heart, you will always find yourself betrothed to the Lover of your soul.

When we enter into a personal relationship with Jesus Christ, we also engage ourselves into a marriage covenant of faith. In Hebrew, this is called a *"ketubah,"* which is a marital contract and an integral part of a traditional Jewish marriage. Christ also refers to the Body of believers as the "Bride," and He is the Bridegroom. Jesus will one day return to collect His readied Bride, and we will return with our Bridegroom to our eternal heavenly address.

In the scripture above, Jesus took with Him the readied "Bride" to the marriage banquet and then shut the door. The five other virgins were not proficient in their preparedness, as they were out shopping for oil to fill their empty lamps. Not only were they were not invited, they were unknown by Him. Jesus will return one day to receive us as His Bride, but we must be accessible, attainable, and equipped for such a time. We are married through our covenant of faith as the efficacy of being chosen by God ties the knot. You are called to be ready and prepared, as you watch and pray for that glorious day.

Action Step of Faith: Be ever so vigilant to be prayerful as you stay connected to your Savior. When you read your Bible, allow Jesus to reveal Himself to you through His Word. Journal what you hear from the Spirit, as you are vigilant to stay awake and prepare for that arrival day to come.

~~~~~~~~~~~~~~

Dear Jesus, You, alone are the Lover of my soul and the Keeper of my heart. Lord, I want to know You more and draw closer each day. Help me to be still and know that You are God alone (Psalm 46:10). May I always bask in the glory of Your presence as I draw closer to Your beating heart. Amen.

_____
_____
_____
_____
_____
_____
_____
_____
_____
_____
_____
_____
_____
_____
_____
_____
_____
_____
_____
_____
_____

DAY
12

*The apostles said to the Lord, "Increase our
faith!" And the Lord said, "If you had faith like
a mustard seed, you would say to this mulberry
tree, 'Be uprooted and be planted in the sea';
and it would obey you."*

—Luke 17:5–6 NASB

*I*n the times of Jesus, a mustard seed was considered to be the
smallest of seeds, but it produced a large plant with a growth
span of up to nine feet tall. This massive tree originated from the
tiniest of beginnings. Looks can be so deceiving!

How many times do you question your faith and placement
in the Kingdom of God? Do you ever feel that your spiritual maturity doesn't measure up to those who have been saved longer than
you? Jesus isn't looking for perfect vessels, but yielded ones. We all
have a place of inception from where we gather our spiritual nutri-
ents to prosper our faith walk. Time is not a specific measurement
stick, as some vines flourish faster than others regardless of the
scattered grain.

The Gospel of Jesus Christ was originally spread by twelve
men who were dedicated to the cause of the Great Commission.
This obedient "Band of Brothers" began as the first seed planters
to eventually cultivate a thriving harvest throughout the world.
Our Lord guides us to initiate sowing, as we are called to germinate
our small seeds of full faith, repentance, passion, and revival, and
then we reap the crop for salvation's sake.

Action Step of Faith: How do you keep yourself watered in dry seasons so your seeds of faith don't wither and die? Spend time reading the Bible and then allow God to place a specific scripture, a *rhema* word, on your heart for that day. Meditate on what the Lord is speaking into your life so as to encourage your growth in this season of holy cultivation.

~~~~~~~~~~~~~~~

Lord, You alone are the Gardener of my soul, as I pray for You to tend to the soil of my heart. In the dry times of my life, may Your living waters saturate me afresh and anew. I desire to blossom into a beautiful flower that sings praises to Your name, while establishing strong roots under Your radiant beam. Amen.

DAY 13

"Be still, and know that I am God! I will be honored by every nation. I will be honored throughout the world."

—Psalm 46:10 NLT

~~~~~~~~~~~~~~

*I*n my life, I have learned the discipline, along with the consequences, of battling myself. Truth be told, I am still known to go a couple of rounds here and there until the Lord reminds me that the battle has already been won on my behalf. When I surrender the battleground and leave my weapons behind, I can feel God ushering me into a blessed respite. In the stillness of your retreat will hinge a mighty victory when you raise your white flag of submission.

The "stillness" the psalmist is capturing in this text is a cease to battle, a time to retire the struggle and release the conflict to the Lord. It is a time to fully renounce the issues and fully rest in His arms. You don't have to journey a distance to find peace! Instead, Jesus invites you to enter into His presence as you meditate in the atmosphere of His love.

The Lord beckons you to the secret place, where you can be still and trust God to inhabit that space with you. As you seek God in that quiet place, He will begin to wash the disdain from your eyes and the unrest from your soul. In the hidden place of the Lord, He will protect you from trouble and surround you with His songs of deliverance (Psalm 32:7).

Action Step of Faith: Today, define what you are ready to yield to the Lord in exchange for a transcendent reservoir of peace over your mind, body, and spirit.

~~~~~~~~~~~~~~

God of Shalom, I submit myself to the altar of grace, where the rivers of Your serenity flow. I pray that You wash over me so I can be a reflection of Your goodness. I seek to find the still waters touching my toes and green pastures at my fingertips where the peaceful winds blow. Amen.

_____

_____

_____

_____

_____

_____

_____

_____

_____

_____

_____

_____

_____

_____

_____

_____

_____

_____

_____

_____

_____

_____

_____

_____

DAY 14

So Elisha left him and went back. He took his
yoke of oxen and slaughtered them. He burned
the plowing equipment to cook the meat and
gave it to the people, and they ate. Then he set
out to follow Elijah and became his servant.

—1 Kings 19:21 NIV

~~~~~~~~~~~~~~

*I*n order to truly close the door to your past life, you must
remove the rock of temptation that comes with the connection
to former interactions. How often do we hold on to past ventures,
careers, relationships, and interventions that prevent our forward
mobility? A safety net is often chock-full of holes of unfulfilled
promises, damaging deceptions, and a bounty of indecision. A
closed door will only allow a new window of possibilities to avail
itself. Holding on to the past will stifle your future, which hinders
your motivation for a new plan and purpose. Sometimes we just
have to toss the rock from the crack in the door, block a number,
pound the career pavement, or dump the pills as we trust God's
ultimate objective!

We find Elisha in the fields of his wealthy father, Shaphat,
plowing and tending to his oxen as his daily duty. Elijah visits with
Elisha, and in that moment, he places a "cloak of change" upon
his broad shoulders. He was preparing all along for a deeper purpose to serve the Lord in those fields of grace. Inadvertently, Elisha
would have to literally burn his plow and have a grand barbecue
for all his people in order to leave his past behind and walk into his
calling. What are you willing to walk away from so you can move
freely into your God-given destiny?

Action Step of Faith: As a child of God, you have been called "chosen," and the Holy Spirit is Your navigational guide for attainment. Claim your inheritance of a good plan for hope and a prosperous future. You might just have to burn some old fences that are blocking your way forward.

~~~~~~~~~~~~~~

Holy Spirit, may Your counsel and guidance in my life's vocation led me to successful pathways. Help me to see past my own agenda, so I can walk faithfully without dependency on my sight. I pray to release what keeps me rutted and bound, as I seek Your mighty hand of mercy, freedom, and providence instead. Amen.

_____
_____
_____
_____
_____
_____
_____
_____
_____
_____
_____
_____
_____
_____
_____
_____
_____
_____
_____
_____

*But you are a chosen race, a royal priesthood, a
holy nation, a people for his own possession, that
you may proclaim the excellencies of him who
called you out of darkness into his marvelous light.*
—1 Peter 2:9 ESV

I would never have been defined as an athlete in my younger days.
I remember waiting for my name to be called in gym class to be
chosen for someone's team, but usually I was a last draft choice. At
times, not being called upon by your peers can create some roots of
rejection, as well as feeling unwanted, unaccepted, or even undesir-
able. This can establish a root of abandonment when you feel disposable by a society that defines you as not good enough! So many of
our young people today have experienced feeling forsaken from their
classmates, and they have resorted to cutting or suicidal ideations.

Jesus chose us before the foundation of this world, so that we
would be holy and without blemish before Him in love (Ephesians
1:4). When we call upon Jesus to reside in our heart, we are never
found abandoned by Him, unlike we might be by the culture of
this world. He fashions us with a desire to be more like Him whom
the world despises. You are a coheir to the throne as your heavenly
Father assigned your allotment to His holy inheritance. Jesus was
rejected, but His eyes were fixed on heaven's ultimate plan.

Throughout your life experiences, how has rejection shaped
your relationships with others in your family, the workplace, in other
relationships, and with God? Has this pain created an atmosphere to
posture in defense before allowing others to get close to you? To draw
closer to God requires the ability to trust Him with your life, as only
He can massage the broken heart of dismissal. Jesus desires to break
the bondage of being spurned or repudiated by a cruel culture since
we were designed for fellowship. To be known by God is to be shel-
tered under His mighty wing of protection, care, and inclusiveness.

Action Step of Faith: Journal your pathway of rejection so you can recognize the root of its ugly inception. Trust God to eradicate the lies from the past, from when you didn't measure up to another's standards. Begin to see yourself in the reflection of the Lord's eyes, knowing that you are always beautiful and acceptable in His sight.

~~~~~~~~~~~~~

God of Everlasting Love, I pray that You would come into my heart and shine Your light into the darkened places of my deepest hurts. Lord, help me to release the pain of past rejections in exchange for the truth of who You say I am! May Your voice be louder than any other so I can receive Your promises of abundant joy. Amen.

_____

_____

_____

_____

_____

_____

_____

_____

_____

_____

_____

_____

_____

_____

_____

_____

_____

_____

_____

_____

_____

DAY 16

But you, beloved, building yourselves up in your most holy faith and praying in the Holy Spirit, keep yourselves in the love of God, waiting for the mercy of our Lord Jesus Christ that leads to eternal life.

—Jude 1:20–21 ESV

- - - - - - - - - - - - -

*I*n the last five years, I have spent many hours exercising my muscles in the gym. I have also employed trainers to partner with me so I can achieve a desired outcome. I needed to build myself up with those who were experienced, dedicated to their craft, and actively teaching others to gain physical excellence. I endeavored to attain a healthier body by practicing daily disciplines, as I was laser-focused on my desired end result.

Our faith can be paralleled in this same thought process. We need to build ourselves up each day with our spiritual muscles. Our regimen should include exercising our holy habits of prayer, fasting, waiting, meditating, and watching in preparation for the Lord of Hosts. We should surround ourselves with those who are like-minded, as we join together in our spiritual development spurring one another on.

Do you pray in the Spirit and allow the movement of His guidance to flow within your voice? This sense of prayer, in harmony with the leading of the Spirit, overrides your own agenda. Have you ever been at a loss for words or even felt you didn't know how to pray? When you allow the Holy Spirit to speak through you, the freedom of a deep, subconscious spiritual awareness can arise. When you keep yourself enveloped in the knowledge of God, you gain a greater capacity for a stronger growth doctrinally, revelation to persevere, and the aptitude to extend your muscle of patience. All roads will lead to an eternal outcome that you will yield through the promise of salvation.

Action Step of Faith: Begin to challenge yourself to pray with the Spirit's lead. Journal your experience, the spoken internal word, and the new depth of attainment that comes with time spent with Jesus. Strengthen your faith muscle in new ways; no pain, no gain!

~~~~~~~~~~~~~~

Faithful Jesus, I desire Your Spirit to engage my prayer life as I dive deeper into Your overwhelming love! God, You alone are my cornerstone! May You construct strong foundations in my prayer life, formed by Your love, ordered by Your steps, and embedded upon the altar of my heart. Amen.

We are here for only a moment, visitors and strangers in the land as our ancestors were before us. Our days on earth are like a passing shadow, gone so soon without a trace.
　　　　　　　　　—1 Chronicles 29:15 NLT

*H*ave you ever felt like a circle in a square in certain places, or environments in which you have been throughout your life? Well, I have experienced that in many different social circles, especially after being saved by Christ. Many of my peers either didn't understand my "new self" or they didn't care to stick around to gain insight. As I was a new creature in Christ, that seemed to provoke conversations with negative connotations. At times, I felt unwanted or left out, but I realized there were other social circles that my spirit recognized as common denominators that were not of this world.

When you feel that you don't necessarily fit in, Jesus says that is because you don't. The Bible compares us to "aliens" and "strangers," just as our ancestors were who walked this planet before us. Our final destination is Heaven, and we are just passing by here until we arrive at our eternal zip code. We are called to bring the light to the dark places, which are spaces that feel foreign since we are temporary residents.

The next time you feel left out, remember that Jesus is always with you, regardless of where you are! Take account of your sphere of influence, and whether it is edifying to your Christian witness. Jesus sticks closer than a brother, and His Spirit resides within you, no matter the company of a jeering crowd.

Action Step of Faith: If you are often placed in a position of compromising your beliefs, watching your language, and avoiding overt gossip, it might be time to make some permanent changes with regard to your social circle. Become more cognizant of your surroundings in order to reflect the heart of God to this perishing culture, not the other way around.

~~~~~~~~~~~~~~

Holy God, today I seek Your magnifying presence around me so that I never desire anything other than Your heavenly oxygen. Lord, I pray for an increase of godly friendships along this momentary journey. Allow my awareness of being a sojourner on this earth become a consecrated confirmation of my dependency to press ever closer to You. Amen.

_____

_____

_____

_____

_____

_____

_____

_____

_____

_____

_____

_____

_____

_____

_____

_____

_____

_____

DAY 18

Keep me as the apple of your eye; hide me in the
shadow of your wings.

—Psalm 17:8 NIV

~~~~~~~~~~~~~~

*H*ow often do we have endearing terms for our children that are personal in nature? Or perhaps for you, it might be a nickname for a spouse or furry friend! Nonetheless, such names are personal and intimate due to your relationship of love, trust, and affiliation of familial standing.

In this verse, we read the psalmist's request for God to keep His gaze upon him and to never lose sight of David's reflection in His pupils. He also beckoned to be kept safe under His mighty arm as a doting parent would do. David deeply desired for His heavenly Father to gaze upon Him with an everlasting love, as He kept him protected and adored as a grand object of affection. The word "keep" in the Hebrew here translates to "hedge about" and "to protect." David's deep yearning was for the Lord's complete attention and affection to preserve him until the day of his vindication.

Do you know that you are the "apple" of your Abba Father's eye? Can you sense His loving arms around you as He prepares a table for you in the presence of your enemies (Psalm 23:5)? When others rebuke you, is your natural reflex to pursue refuge under the wing of God's mercy and grace? He awaits You with open arms! He is a loving heavenly Father, even when a biological parent might not have been equipped to do so. For some, it might take your adulthood to heal your childhood. Take heart, for with God all things are possible (Matthew 19:26).

Action Step of Faith: Seek God when others leave you high and dry before you begin set to up camp in a dark cavern. Bask in the embodied presence of the Holy Spirit, who always has you in His foresight and not His hindsight.

〜〜〜〜〜〜〜〜〜〜〜〜

El Roi, the God who sees me, regardless of where I might try to hide from my accusers, today I pray to be covered by You alone. O Lord who delights in me, as a Father reveres His offspring with adoration, assist me to recognize You right next to me. Amen.

_____

_____

_____

_____

_____

_____

_____

_____

_____

_____

_____

_____

_____

_____

_____

_____

_____

_____

_____

_____

_____

_____

_____

*Jesus answered them, "Do you finally believe? In
fact, you're about to make a run for it—saving
your own skins and abandoning me. But I'm not
abandoned. The Father is with me. I've told you
all this so that trusting me, you will be unshakable and assured, deeply at peace. In this godless
world you will continue to experience difficulties.
But take heart! I've conquered the world."*
—John 16:33 MSG

~~~~~~~~~~~~~~

*H*eadlines blare as we read about pestilence of disease, plagues of civil unrest, and devastating violence with destructive consequences. In the time that you had to quarantine during the COVID-19 crisis of 2020, did you lean into Jesus or bend in the other direction? Was your impulse to shake in fear or stand in faith? How has your capacity to remain consistently trusting in God been tethered throughout that year of clear vision?

Those were a lot of ponder points to reveal your wellness potential in times of unprecedented trials and tribulations. Actually, you are not alone since the disciples were also looking for an escape route when situations became heated and dangerous. But Jesus reminded them that with Him by their side, they were never alone, and they would be soaked in peace as they rose up unshakable! The same is true for you and for me! We are called to be encouraged by this Good News to remain steady in our confident hope in Christ.

Jesus also reminds us in this verse that in this world we will have trouble, but we must remember that He alone overcame this world by His resurrection. As a covenant believer, we share the promise of life everlasting, as Jesus conquered death through His victory in the empty tomb.

Action Step of Faith: Beloved, is it well with your soul? Name your fear so you can claim victory over it with intentional definition. Place it in the mighty hands of God so you can reclaim your peace, no matter the matter!

~~~~~~~~~~~~~~~

Loving Lord, I beseech You to remove my fear and worry in exchange for Your peace engulfed with joy! I have spent too much time running from what haunts my days and nights, as it robs my sleep and health. Jesus, today I declare in Your majestic name, that I will surrender these schemes of the enemy at your footstool so I can grasp the gift of Your holy tranquility. Amen.

_____

_____

_____

_____

_____

_____

_____

_____

_____

_____

_____

_____

_____

_____

_____

_____

_____

_____

_____

_____

*Do not be deceived: God is not mocked, for
whatever one sows, that will he also reap. For
the one who sows to his own flesh will from the
flesh reap corruption, but the one who sows to
the Spirit will from the Spirit reap eternal life.*
—Galatians 6:7–8 ESV

A "known" life in Christ is a "sown" life, lived intentionally to please God. We are expected to "scatter our
seeds" of an authentic Christian witness reflective of our daily lifestyle. Then, we will be more effective to garner disciples for Jesus
when we cross-pollinate with both believers and non-believers. It is
important to take stock of our disciplines daily to be sure that we
are reaping for Kingdom causes and not worldly applauses.

The apostle Paul is reminding us that reaping is the blessed
outcome of eternal life when we sow our lives to the Spirit. How
often do we get knocked off course and scatter our seeds on hardened soil or rocky dirt? What kind of garden do you pursue to harvest, and what will you gain by throwing your grain to the wind?

We need to remember that the Gardener of our soil desires
to tend to our garden with abundant blessings of living water and
His "Son" shining upon us. Beloved, do you know the love of the
Master Gardener? He jealously vies for your affection and attention as your faith walk increases ever so infinitely. God desires you
to desire Him above all other enticing grounds. Stay in love with
the Lord to avoid wandering off into an uncharted wilderness.

Action Step of Faith: How often do you find yourself distant from God? Are you able to draw closer to Him, even if you are not reaping in holy spaces? Call upon the Holy Spirit to guide you back on the road to a repentant landing with holy standing!

~~~~~~~~~~~~~~~

Forgiving Lord, I thank you for Your love, which is lavished upon me each day. I pray to reciprocate that adoration with each syllable that is spoken from my lips. Help me to desire Your dwelling place of grace beyond any deceptive spaces that might attempt to lure me away from You. Amen.

DAY 21

"When you pass through the waters, I will be with you; and when you pass through the rivers, they will not sweep over you. When you walk through the fire, you will not be burned; the flames will not set you ablaze."
—Isaiah 43:2 NIV

I don't know about you, but I am not a proficient swimmer. When I attempt to go in the water, a floatation device is usually within reach. I know to always wear my life preserver when boating, so I won't be immersed in the water and will remain on course.

When we travel in deep and tumultuous rivers that have strong and unwavering currents, Jesus is our lifeboat. We should always have faith in Him as our rescuer, whether it be rough seas, gusty winds, or overwhelming waves that try to submerge us to the bottom floor. Jesus will always pull us from the overpowering breakers, as He will deliver from the raging waves of our circumstances. He is the only One who can speak peace to the wind and cause the floodwaters of our soul to recede.

Can you place your trust in the Lord when you are drowning in seas of homelessness, financial disarray, broken relationships, or an unfavorable doctor's report? What is your ability to place your hand in the One who created yours? Can you remain resilient as you stay afloat with your cognizance that Jesus is with you no matter the storm within?

Action Step of Faith: As a child of God, allow yourself to be more aware that Jesus is with you in the storms of your life as He is Your true buoyant hope. Invite Him into the struggles that you are facing because He never abandons the "ship of your heart"!

~~~~~~~~~~~~~~~

Precious Lord, help me to lean on You when I am overwhelmed with issues and problems that overtake my drowning thoughts. I pray not to depend on my own understanding when situations falter, but to trust You for the direct route for my life's voyage (Proverbs 3:5). Amen.

_____

_____

_____

_____

_____

_____

_____

_____

_____

_____

_____

_____

_____

_____

_____

_____

_____

_____

_____

_____

_____

_____

_____

_____

*"I will be your Father, and you will be my sons
and daughters," declares the Lord Almighty.*
—2 Corinthians 6:18 isv

~ ~ ~ ~ ~ ~ ~ ~ ~ ~ ~ ~ ~ ~

*T*here is something so loving and personal about a father claiming his relational connection to his children. Unfortunately, in our culture, we are seeing a diversion away from fathers being present in the home and more matriarchal family lead structures erupting. As a woman who was a single parent, I recognize the lasting effects this can have on children as they try to fill a void of a paternal voice. But there has also been a paradigm shift on the flipside of a vacant maternal presence, too. This was never the intended design of the family unit by God, but our culture affirms otherwise.

Our heavenly Father reconciles us as His children who are partakers of a personal relationship with Him. We are adopted into the family of Christ when we invite Jesus to take ownership of our heart. He is the Father of the fatherless and the motherless children (Psalm 68:5). Each one will never be abandoned by our Holy Father but reclaimed by His everlasting love to be heirs to His throne.

Beloved of Christ, have you ever felt disposable by your parents or someone who raised you? Has that left an indelible mark of hurt, rejection, or anger on your heart? Our Abba Father in heaven signs off on our adoption papers as we are eternally recognized as part of His royal family tree. The awareness of belonging to the ancestry of Christ is the first eraser to the scars of your past invalidations for those who call upon His name.

Action Step of Faith: Reconfigure your family tree today where your point of origin begins at your "rebirth" in Christ. If you need to take an inventory of where your roots of disconnection began, reconnect with the One who loved you first. Count this to be the first leaf revealed in your newfound genealogy.

~~~~~~~~~~~~~~~

Abba Father, may You come into my heart like a flood as You wash my mind clean from past offenses, hurts, and rebukes. Lord, be my parental caretaker so that I may fully cast my cares on the Holy One who renames me "accepted, adopted, and adored." Amen.

_____
_____
_____
_____
_____
_____
_____
_____
_____
_____
_____
_____
_____
_____
_____
_____
_____
_____
_____
_____

DAY
23

*"Come to me, all you who are weary and bur-
dened, and I will give you rest. Take my yoke
upon you and learn from me, for I am gentle
and humble in heart, and you will find rest for
your souls. For my yoke is easy and my burden
is light."*

—Matthew 11:28–30 NIV

*H*ave you ever felt the weight of the world lying upon your
shoulders? Perhaps the heaviness of all that you are carrying actually creates physical pain in your neck! For me, when
I am overwhelmed, overburdened, and just plain overdone, my
entire physique begins to feel laden down, and this is evidenced by
my posture. I believe God designed us to stand upright as we are
instructed to cast our burdens upon His capable shoulders.

Jesus is personally inviting us to trust Him with our arduous problems and the exhausting circumstances in our lives. Jesus
has even a deeper, longer reaching desire to provide "rest for your
weary soul." The yoke of this world that binds us to sin is expunged
through the redemptive work that was finished at Calvary's cross.
We can acquire rest that is solidified through the promises in Jesus
Christ when we commit our souls unto Him.

Are you feeling weary or tired these days? Perhaps you have
been for years? What is the barrier preventing you from trusting
God with managing your overload of trouble? Jesus' desire is for
us to live a life of abundance, even in trials and tribulations. When
we walk with Him, He carries us, even when we can't stand up. We
must learn the discipline of falling backward into the Lord's arms
as He catches us before we plummet into the darkened pitfalls of
this life.

Action Step of Faith: Beloved, what burden are you carrying today that you can begin to release into the arms of Christ? Begin to pray specifically for the shift from your weary hand into the Lord's available one. Let this be a new posture of holy "modus operandi"!

~ ~ ~ ~ ~ ~ ~ ~ ~ ~ ~ ~ ~ ~

Merciful God, prayerfully I entrust to You my afflicted soul, unto Your wellspring of peace. Adonai, teach me to walk by faith and not by sight so I will not stumble and fall, but so that I will rest to be ever so blessed (2 Corinthians 5:7). Amen.

DAY 24

"But when the Father sends the Advocate as my representative—that is, the Holy Spirit—he will teach you everything and will remind you of everything I have told you."
—John 14:26 NLT

~~~~~~~~~~~~~~

*H*ow often do you require some extra help? Throughout the course of my life, I have struggled with comprehension. I can remember as far back as grade school, instructors keeping me after class to review questions that I missed answering. Specifically, this was due to my inability to grasp proper recall. As an adult, I began to master the discipline of note taking and highlighting to sharpen my perception of memory to successful retention.

To skew this biblically, Jesus was explaining to the disciples that He needed to leave them so the Holy Spirit, His indwelling representative, would come to be their Helper. For all that Jesus taught them, the Advocate would jog their memory so they could spread the Gospel accurately and proficiently with the Spirit's lead. Jesus resides within us, and He is our holy GPS, God Positioning System, so we never lose sight of His truth via His Word.

Many of us find it challenging to read the Bible, so many just do not. How often have you started in Genesis and found yourself frustrated by the time you arrived at Leviticus? To know God is to know Him through His holy Word. Jesus reveals Himself to us through the pages of the Scriptures and the Psalms. The Bible was not meant to be read as a full meal! We are to take small bites and chew on each word, as the Holy Spirit assists in our thorough digestion.

Action Step of Faith: Let this be the year you start at Genesis and go completely through to Revelation. Take your time, and invite the Holy Spirit to travel along this journey with you, until arriving at your final destination of true understanding. It's not a race, but a lifelong journey to fully glean the Good News!

~~~~~~~~~~~~~~

Gracious God, I thank You for the Personhood of the Holy Spirit, who guides me and teaches me throughout my life. Lord, I pray for Your Word to be a light unto my path and a lamp unto my feet so I may never stray from you (Psalm 119:105). My desire is to live according to Your inspired Word as You inscribe it on my all-embracing heart, mind, and soul. Amen.

DAY 25

Therefore, brothers, since we have confidence to enter the holy places by the blood of Jesus, by the new and living way that he opened for us through the curtain, that is, through his flesh, and since we have a great priest over the house of God, let us draw near with a true heart in full assurance of faith, with our hearts sprinkled clean from an evil conscience and our bodies washed with pure water.

—Hebrews 10:19–22 ESV

*H*ave you ever looked at life from the outside in? Perhaps you weren't part of the "in crowd," or your family situation didn't fit the mold of another's specific design. Have you ever felt judged by a jury of your peers before you even were provided a chance to plead your case?

As a single parent for many years, I recall those who excluded me because of my divorced "singleness." This affected their status quo definition of what a parental unit should be and caused some unwelcomed opinions, as well. Thankfully, there were those who loved me, as they supported us through those tenuous, painful, and challenging years. Time taught me well, as it ushered me into a pit where I would discover my eternal destination. Christ was hovering in my circumference, while waiting for me to call upon His name.

This Scripture reminds us that as the curtain was torn, so was His body, hanging upon Golgotha's hill. We always have access to approach Jesus with confidence as He desires us to draw near. The veil of the heavenly tabernacle is continually open due to the sanctifying work of Christ. As Christians, we can live with full assurance of the promise that our hearts are cleansed by His purifying sacrifice.

We are to prostrate ourselves before the Lord, offering our full cup of repentance in return for His forgiveness, mercy, and grace.

You are not part of a trend-setting club, but you have an eternal relationship that offers a kinship with the Body of Christ. Beloved, no matter your situation in life, you can operate by faith to effectuate a view from the inside out! We will always find acceptance in the arms of our Savior!

Action Step of Faith: Where do you fit in these days? Let this be the beginning of surrounding yourself not with quantity, but with quality social circles that share commonalities of faith. Be certain that God is in the center of your friendships so they will stand firm when life does not.

～～～～～～～～～～～～～

Gracious Savior, prayerfully assign me friends for this journey of life. At times I struggle with feeling lonely and unaccepted, but I know that when I call upon Your name You alone hide me under Your wing of love. Reveal to my spirit those social connections that will bring healthy companionship and genuine friendship into my life. Amen.

_____
_____
_____
_____
_____
_____
_____
_____
_____
_____
_____
_____
_____

"As the Father has loved me, so have I loved you. Abide in my love."

—John 15:9 ESV

Not everything in this world is mutually exclusive, especially within relationships. What we deposit into our inter-connected affiliations with others doesn't always have an equal return. Sometimes we might break even, other times it could produce an overdraft, while bankruptcy of the heart can be the final determination.

Jesus reminds us that when we abide with Him daily in an active posture of relationship, He mutually abides in us. In order for our kinship to flourish, it must be tended to each day. The lush gardens require daily watering, a bounty of sunshine, and attentive care, or they will wither away. Our personal intimacy with Jesus calls us into persistent postures, as we unceasingly seek His presence, or it shall surely fade, as well. The word *abide* means to remain fixed or stable in a state of love that is continually with Him all of our days.

Do you abide with Jesus each day so you can feel Him abound within your soul? It is in the mutual adoration between you and Christ that His love deepens and prospers in your action of faith. Jesus forewarned us of troubled times, but because of our active pursuit of His love, we shall receive peace even if our hearts become shattered! The only true dependent relationship that we should ever engage in is with our Lord; otherwise, it's a recipe for codependency. When you function in a bond that is solely contingent on another human being, that will eventually usurp your relationship with God. Put God first, or there will be nothing left spiritually to be dispersed.

Action Step of Faith: Are your relationships evenly distributed? Do you tend to give more than you receive, or vice versa? The first relationship that needs to always be favored is your relationship with God. Only then can you actively perpetuate whole and healthy relationships in your life. Take inventory of the priority list of your daily connections; be aware of where God is found on your roll!

~~~~~~~~~~~~~~

Abba Father, I pray to seek You first as my prominent and most honored relationship. Lord Jesus, I strive to place You above all others so that the initial beginning of my day, my time, and my heart belong to my first true love. Holy Spirit, help me to establish relational boundaries with darkened lines so that I can recognize healthy ones. Amen.

Since, then, you have been raised with Christ,
set your hearts on things above, where Christ is,
seated at the right hand of God. Set your minds
on things above, not on earthly things. For you
died, and your life is now hidden with Christ
in God.

—Colossians 3:1–3 NIV

----

*D*o you remember playing the game hide-and-seek as a
young child? I wonder how many children today in our
culture would even recognize this activity. It involved hiding somewhere creative so no one would find you. In some cases, if you
were a really proficient "hider," the game could be quite exten-
sive. However, the object was to remain hidden from the one who
searched for you in a very intentional pursuit. But the object is
always to be eventually found.

This can sometimes imitate our life's quest. We hide ourselves away from the things that we fear, that bring us anxiety and
contempt. But in that same breath, do we hide ourselves from
the Holy One who desires to be our mighty Protector? Child of
the Most-High, do you evade the shelter of God in the midst of
stormy turbulence, or do you pursue the secret place of His love
for refuge?

If you died with Christ to live again in Him, you no longer
have to run, because Jehovah Nissi is your Defender. You must
learn the discipline to keep your eyes focused upon heavenly realms
and not earthly matters. God is the perfect concealing place as you
now can dwell under His wings of secured grace. He will hide you
in His shelter in the day of trouble; He will conceal you under the
covering of His tent; He will lift you upon a rock (Psalm 27:5).

Action Step of Faith: Take stock of where your building blocks of trust began to falter. Today, start to reconstruct your relationship with the Lord, as your faith will rise up, built firmly by faith, cemented in trust, and permeated with hope.

~~~~~~~~~~~~~~~

Loving God, teach me to seek You first, as I am Your held lamb. Help me to supernaturally understand my new life, hidden in Your arms of holy protection every waking hour. Amen.

_____

_____

_____

_____

_____

_____

_____

_____

_____

_____

_____

_____

_____

_____

_____

_____

_____

_____

_____

_____

_____

_____

_____

DAY 28

Make me to know your ways, O LORD; teach
me your paths. Lead me in your truth and teach
me, for you are the God of my salvation; for you
I wait all the day long.

—Psalm 25:4–5 ESV

~~~~~~~~~~~~~~

As a younger girl, I can recall playing a game called Truth or Dare. The premise was either to typically answer a provocative question or take an even more exasperating dare. What were we thinking, calling this an enjoyable pastime? However, why wouldn't we just choose the truth, since it was our own, as opposed to a dangerous dare? As a society, we need to relish our truth, even if the "dares" of life have led us into sin.

This psalter prompts us to lean upon the Lord's guidance, so we can garner a better understanding about the manner of lifestyle He so yearns for us to have. Jesus is our lifelong Teacher, who put on flesh to model virtues for us to shadow and reflect. When we walk in tandem with the Lord, we can wait in His holy presence to ascertain the truth of His Word and His way.

Are you able to bask in His glory to know that Jesus Christ is the Way, the Truth, and the Life (John 14:6)? There exists no other entryway unto the Father for our salvation. Seeking God in this hour and being still before Him will enable you to gain profitable insight into His truth and His written word. Make time to remain in the glory of His manifest Spirit, as there is no other place on earth worth tarrying for.

Action Step of Faith: It is so important to always remain a "teachable spirit." Every day you spend time in His distinct company, there is always an opportunity for instruction and counsel. In the stillness of that moment, take time to listen and capture all that the Lord is conveying to you.

~~~~~~~~~~~~~~

Master, Teacher, come and show me new things that I have never seen or heard before. As I enter the secret place of my heart, where only You reside, help me to gain godly knowledge of the pathway for my life. Amen.

*But God demonstrates his own love for us in
this: While we were still sinners, Christ died for
us.*

—Romans 5:8 NIV

~~~~~~~~~~~~~~

Throughout our lifetimes, people will come and go. Some will stay for the long haul, while others will depart once situations become either too challenging or no longer beneficial. The pause for the cause of intimacy can be measured by the valiant effort for another to prevail through the fatalities of life. However, only one relationship will endure through it all: our relationship with Jesus Christ. When we are known by our Father, He stays in close proximity to us as we need to remain in Him (John 15:4).

Christ did not die for righteous individuals, or for good "doers," but for those who have sinned against Him. It is through Christ's death, on our behalf, that God demonstrates His love for us, no matter the pit in which we have plummeted. Jesus doesn't bail out or forsake us when our zip code moves to the fringes of society. He extends to us an uplifted hand and unending love with a choice to vacate our pits of destruction.

We are all sinners saved by His grace, and only by the shed blood of Christ can we be redeemed. Have you personally experienced the demonstrative love of the Father in the deepest action of your sin? God desires to take your sins upon the words of your confession and submerge them in the deepest sea of forgetfulness. Are you willing to repent with a full heart so you can be reconciled with Christ? You can only experience a revived heart through the conduit of a repentant one.

Action Step of Faith: Do you live your life knowing that you are forgiven and loved by God? When was the last time you laid down your full cup of repentance before the Lord? Let today be the day of sanctification unto confessing your sins before the Holy One, who alone can fully forgive.

~~~~~~~~~~~~~~

Father God, I come before You as a sinner saved by grace, and I ask for forgiveness. Lord, help me to place my transgressions at Your footstool so I may once again walk in the reconciled freedom that You desire for my life. Thank You, O Lord, as You are forever good and faithful! Amen.

_____
_____
_____
_____
_____
_____
_____
_____
_____
_____
_____
_____
_____
_____
_____
_____
_____
_____
_____

DAY
30

And I am certain that God, who began the good work within you, will continue his work until it is finally finished on the day when Christ Jesus returns.

—Philippians 1:6 NLT

~ ~ ~ ~ ~ ~ ~ ~ ~ ~ ~ ~ ~ ~

*H*ow often do we start projects but never complete them? At the time, our intensity is laser-focused with a heightened measure of adrenaline pumping with conviction through our veins. At what point does the proverbial "air" become "deflated" from the "tire" of our desire? Our completion is manifested through the equipping of the Holy Spirit, who will guide us to our glorious fulfillment.

The apostle Paul is bringing a message of blessed assurance that God's promises will most likely outlast our commitments to Him. God's desire for His children is to finish the good work He began in us to completion to endeavor a finish line acquisition. Authentic spiritual progress is embedded in what God has done, is doing, and will continue to do. His faithfulness is an enduring one that will prevail until Jesus returns. God's love will keep us engaged as we persevere on this narrow road.

What is the point of retrieval at which you don't complete what you began? Jesus designed you to hold on to Him in times of need as you traverse the unnavigated landscape of your life. As a King's kid, Jesus reminds us not to grow weary in doing good, as in due time we will reap a mighty harvest (Galatians 6:9). When we stay the course, the benefits will outweigh the cost, as Jesus paid it all on our behalf!

Action Step of Faith: Take account of where you are in your life's call. Can you recognize a pattern of "starts and stops" along the way? As a believer, take this time in prayer to seek God's calling for your life and begin to take stock of how you can regain your holy edge for attainment before continuing to the next thirty days. As we began, journal your progress forward, so you can create changes as you have a firm foundation in Christ for holy construction to reclaim your transformed life.

~~~~~~~~~~~~~~~

Lord Jesus, forever guide me along this broken road as You call me Yours. Help me to discern clear direction at the crossroads of resolutions, alternatives, and solutions. I pray to personify Godly wisdom to procure Your greater purpose for me on earth, until I reach my Heaven-bound home. Holy Spirit, breathe upon me so I may withstand any distractions that might thwart Your good plan! Amen.

A "Transformed Life" in Christ the Next 30 Days

DAY 31

Don't become so well-adjusted to your culture that you fit into it without even thinking. Instead, fix your attention on God. You'll be changed from the inside out. Readily recognize what he wants from you, and quickly respond to it. Unlike the culture around you, always dragging you down to its level of immaturity, God brings the best out of you, develops well-formed maturity in you.
—Romans 12:2 MSG

- - - - - - - - - - - - - -

*B*ack in the day, I recall spending time with my kids putting puzzles together. I remember this one puzzle that had over a thousand pieces, and most of them resembled one another. I also recall painstakingly trying to place some pieces where they appeared to fit, but they were just not the right ones. You might compare this to putting a circle in a square, but no matter what you do, that shape won't adjust unless you transform it.

Have you ever experienced such a scenario in your life? The word *transformation* is defined as a thorough or dramatic change in form or appearance. When we invite Jesus Christ into our heart, we, too, experience a dramatic change in our thought process, our priorities, our desires, and our social circles. It truly is a holy make-over! We begin to discern our situations through a Christ-centered lens to uncover the worth of something by putting it to the test by actual practice. To perceive the difference of a godly position in opposition to a world-based criteria.

Have you ever sensed that when you revisit people, places, and various things from the past, it's no longer a pliable fit in your life? As your mind is renewed in Christ, the lens of your heart is adjusted. The yearning for things of this world will cease as the tenets of faith will increase. That is the transformed life in Christ, as we die to our self-indulgences each day. Our puzzle pieces, shaped through our conversion, will be a perfected fit, as we walk out our salvation each day in tandem with God.

Action Step of Faith: How do you define yourself? Is it by your actions or by your words? As a Christian, find a balance of both to be a genuine witness to this culture. Don't look to fit in to the bends of this world, but find your boldness to press into Christ for those who don't yet know the befitting way!

~~~~~~~~~~~~~~~

Father God, guide me in my transformed spirit as I grow each day to reflect Your heart. I pray to seek You each day as I request that I must decrease so You can increase in me (John 3:30). Amen.

DAY 32

I waited patiently for the LORD; and He inclined to me and heard my cry. He brought me up out of the pit of destruction, out of the miry clay, and He set my feet upon a rock making my footsteps firm.

—Psalm 40:1–2 NASB

~~~~~~~~~~~~~~~

*I*n different intervals of life, we might find ourselves deep within a ditch that can be defined by stress, anxiety, fear, bitterness, pride, and despair. Truth be told, that list can be an endless one! The time in that pit can appear endless, as well. How do we vacate that "living grave" of self-destruction? More importantly, how do we have the desire to be rescued, which has been placated by this disillusionment of an uncomfortable, comfort zone of entitled attention?

The psalmist poignantly states that when we wait upon the Lord in a posture of patience, He hears our cries and comes to us. By our heart knowledge of trust, God rescues us from our pits of human wreckage as we hinge our hope upon our Creator. It is the desire of God to hoist His children out of the muck and mire of our worldly existence. Only then can He place our feet steadily on His sturdy rock so we may stand firm when we choose faith over fear.

Are you "sick and tired" of being down and counted out? How often do you invite Jesus Christ into your pit of pity and your miry mess? Why it is that we seem to ponder the thought that we can do this alone? I can recall the dumpsters of demolition remaining from bad choices coupled with even worse attitudes. When we call upon the name of Jesus, He hears our cries and inclines Himself to us. When we fully trust and depend on God's intervention in the trenches of our circumstances, only then can we really abandon the preposterous pit.

Action Step of Faith: What have you embraced that is no longer yours to bear, as it reinstates a local pit address? Journal what you need to relinquish into the hands of Jesus, as you take your first step of ascent out of the disheartening ditch.

~~~~~~~~~~~~~~~

Lord, in Your mercy, help me to yearn for a release of my pit design that I have fashioned for myself. I pray to call upon Your mighty name as You take my hand and begin to position my feet upon Your firm, holy ground. Amen.

_____
_____
_____
_____
_____
_____
_____
_____
_____
_____
_____
_____
_____
_____
_____
_____
_____
_____
_____
_____

DAY
33

*You are my defender and protector; I put my
hope in your promise.*

—Psalm 119:114 GNT

~~~~~~~~~~~~~~~

*H*ave you ever experienced, during times of turbulent relationships, fantasy battles raging inside your mind? If so, then you are familiar with the conjuring up of defensive retorts to those who posture themselves in a place of offense against you. I could have the propensity to prudently prepare for a battle of the tongues! But mine was shut closed when the battle ceased and desisted before my first vowel was formed, as an alternative pleasantry was relayed instead. The energy we expel to defend ourselves could be put to better use when remanded into God's hands and convicted conversation.

God is our Defender, and He goes before us on the frontlines of our minds, bodies, and spirits. The psalmist reminds us here that when we place our trust in God's protection, we can find hope in His promise of our care. The Lord is always with us and watching over us. In Exodus 17:15, Moses built an altar and named it "the Lord is my Banner," or Jehovah Nissi. God showed the nation of Israel that He conquered His enemies on their behalf, as Aaron and Hur supported the arms of Moses.

Can you remember this promise, that God goes before daily combat, unmanaged strife, and troubling encounters so you don't have to engage in warfare? However, call upon Jehovah Nissi in your prayers of warfare, when you are surrounded on all sides. God identifies you as His child, and your label provides an umbrella of protection that is enduring. You are commissioned to spread the Good News of the Gospel, and that banner of Moses is your inheritance of a battlefield victory today! Allow the conviction of the Holy Advocate to speak on your behalf so you can remain silently at ease.

Action Step of Faith: Lay down your weapons of warfare as you bend your knees to the Lord. Invite Jesus into your drama that perpetuates an unnecessary script. Let the Lord stand before you as your Defender so you can rest in His unending peace with a tongue that is no longer lashing.

~~~~~~~~~~~~~~

Loving Lord, help me to surrender my anger, resentment, and grudges I have believed that I am entitled to from hurtful interactions. Please help me to love more than I despise, and draw a line of truce onto my forgiving heart. Amen.

Therefore, if anyone is in Christ [that is, grafted in, joined to Him by faith in Him as Savior], he is a new creature [reborn and renewed by the Holy Spirit]; the old things [the previous moral and spiritual condition] have passed away. Behold, new things have come [because spiritual awakening brings a new life].

—2 Corinthians 5:17 AMP

- - - - - - - - - - - - - -

*S*o often, when we encounter the open door to new opportunities and Spirit-filled possibilities, we gravitate to the ingress of our past entryways. We tend to scribe our new chapters with a dried inkwell from the days gone by in order to pen tomorrow's vision. Looking back at my journey, there have been quantified examples of staying stuck in "lifeless" situations that prevented a revived manifestation for this "new creature" in Christ to thrive. The beginning of my new life with my Great Redeemer was the death of my old, flesh-filled self.

With God all things are possible, especially when we follow our Savior's leading to yield to His ways as newly formed creatures in Christ (Matthew 19:26). As born-again believers, our rebirth delivers us to a redemptive state where we live according to the Spirit as we are destined to reflect Jesus. The former things we once desired begin to perish, as our new moral compass points upward to Kingdom causes with holy pauses.

If you are a newly formed creation in Christ, or if you have been walking with the Lord for many years, do the glory days of old cry out to you at times? How often do the things of the past attempt to slither their way into your present life? Even as saved Christians, the act of self-denial coupled with death to our flesh needs to be a daily discipline. Child of God, take heed, with vigilance, to bask in the presence of the Lord. In this hour, be awakened by the Spirit who dwells within, so you don't fall prey to a past indulgent temptation.

Action Step of Faith: Take stock of your spiritual condition. Are you in need of a jolt of faith or even a rekindled spirit? Beware that you don't fall into a space of complacent faith, but actively seek Jesus each morning. Journal your conversations with Him because they will drift away.

~~~~~~~~~~~~~~

Jesus, my heart pants to sit at Your feet and listen to Your heart beat against my own. I pray to be led by the Spirit, who is alive within me, and to follow ever so closely as You establish my steps. I passionately await the newness of reverent visions and dreams to inspire my daily relationship with You. Amen.

_____

_____

_____

_____

_____

_____

_____

_____

_____

_____

_____

_____

_____

_____

_____

_____

_____

DAY 35

"You are the light of the world—like a city on a hilltop that cannot be hidden. No one lights a lamp and then puts it under a basket. Instead, a lamp is placed on a stand, where it gives light to everyone in the house. In the same way, let your good deeds shine out for all to see, so that everyone will praise your heavenly Father."
—Matthew 5:14–16 NLT

~~~~~~~~~~~~~~

S ome of the rites of passage from my youth were cold lemonade on a warm July day, toasting marshmallows for s'mores, and catching fireflies in my hands. Close your eyes and inhale the "scents" of summers gone by. I remember, even with my boys, capturing lightning bugs and placing them in a jar with a punctured lid for air. Unfortunately, their captivating lights diminished as they couldn't survive while bound in a small area, but instead they longed to be free to spread their illumination in the nocturnal sky.

Jesus desires us to be the "light of this world," which must never be hidden or extinguished. We must shine brightly in those darkened places of divine appointments and shadow-filled spaces so all can find their way home. God desires us to be His matchsticks as we stoke the flame of the Spirit for those whose embers have gone dim! Let all that you do be predicated on Jesus' behalf, as He receives all the honor, glory, and praise!

How brightly do you shine in the midst of so much darkness? Are you a contagious Christian who spreads the fire of God, or do you need to be in the proximity of a holy bonfire? In this life, you will have seasons of ebbing and flowing. If you are mindful of your spiritual lack, then that can give rise to a new flame of the Holy Spirit to burn brightly again.

Action Step of Faith: Seek God in those times of hiding yourself away. You are a precious lamp, and the Spirit is your lampstand, upon which you are to be placed. Be aware of who is dousing your flame and what is feeding the fire of desire in your life. Allow the love of Jesus to be illuminated in your heart so you can once again radiate His all-consuming fire with the oil of the Lord.

~~~~~~~~~~~~~~~~

Lord of the One True Light, shine Your face upon mine as Your love ignites my passion to spread the love of Christ. I pray to be a matchstick to all who are in my proximity, so I might be a useful instrument of Your holy design. Amen.

*So keep your thoughts continually fixed on all
that is authentic and real, honorable and admirable, beautiful and respectful, pure and holy,
merciful and kind. And fasten your thoughts on
every glorious work of God, praising him always.*
—Philippians 4:8 TPT

*M*y mind has had the propensity to run on overdrive at
times. I compare my thoughts to a racecar speeding on
the track, literally reaching ridiculous velocities from 0 to 100 in under
a minute. Well, perhaps that might a bit dramatic, but that is what my
constant looping of analytic self-dialogue can present at times. This
can exist to be our reality in the midst of major relational strife, overwhelming issues, health pandemics, and distortions of worldly views.
Sometimes we just have to pull the speeding vehicle of our minds to
the curb, put ourselves in park, and hand the keys over to Jesus.

Paul reminded the church at Philippi to be encouraged to live
their lives as Jesus intended them to do so. These are instructional
words to grasp, as they kept their minds steady while setting their
gaze upon Jesus. The Philippians' reflective thoughts, coupled by a
manifested Christian lifestyle, would usher them to the finish line
because of their true faith. Successful living was produced by positive thinking, which was foundational in the truth of God's goodness and inspired Word.

Do your thoughts reflect your life of faith? Perhaps the apostle Paul's list of how to sift our mind's eye would be a helpful measurement of our daily reasoning process. Could you take your contemplations and rest them under a holy scope of authentic, real,
honorable, admirable, lovely, respectful, holy, and merciful truths?
You might have to park your speed racer of intellect for a while!
Now might be the time to trade it in for a calmer, steadier, more
peace-filled ride driven by the Holy Spirit.

Action Step of Faith: Pull over today and rest in His Spirit-filled presence of love and mercy. Today, take the unceasing thoughts that haunt you and place them under the blood of Christ, as you praise God in the middle of your wreckage! God desires to saturate your mind and heart with the inspiration to worship Him as you serve others. Park and ride with Jesus today as you rest in His passenger seat of grace!

~~~~~~~~~~~~~~~

Lord Almighty, help me to stop and rest in my mind today. I pray to release all my unhealthy ponderings and analytic mindsets to You. In exchange, dear Lord, grant me peace in any unrest, joy in sadness, and hope in oppression that I may have embraced for way too long. Amen.

_____
_____
_____
_____
_____
_____
_____
_____
_____
_____
_____
_____
_____
_____
_____
_____
_____
_____
_____

DAY
37

*But he said to me, "My grace is sufficient for
you, for my power is made perfect in weakness."
Therefore, I will boast all the more gladly of my
weaknesses, so that the power of Christ may rest
upon me.*

—2 Corinthians 12:9 ESV

~~~~~~~~~~~~~~

*I*n this world, what does "enough" look like? We live in a society that is driven by constant acquisition, where nothing ever
seems fulfilling as to an indelible satisfaction marker. There exists
a missing place inside of us all that can never be filled except by
God. And in that space resides, unequivocally, His sufficiency of
grace that is our oxygen in times of desperation and despair.

In this verse, the apostle Paul indicates the abundance of
God's grace that is poured out upon our lives. It is only through
the Lord, who can move in our weakened state of earthly existence
while working in our spirits to provide rest to our souls. In that
moment, we give God the glory as we lay claim to His goodness
and overflowing affection for our revived condition.

Do you define God as being "enough" in your life? The biblical definition of the word *enough* translates "to satisfy desire, to
rest, or to be quiet." Would this be evident in your relationship
with the Lover of your soul? Can you find rest in God's sufficient
grace in your circumstances today? Construct an altar in your heart
for God to rest His mercy upon. Watch Him begin to demonstrate
His mighty power of sufficient love in your most debilitated and
deconstructed state.

Action Step of Faith: Today allow God to use your weakness for the perfection of His power. Remind yourself that in your weakness, for Christ's sake, He will make you strong, but we need to allow Him entry into our mess (2 Corinthians 12:10). Journal the pathway from your mess to your message, as there is no glory without your story, as that is how you build your testimony!

~~~~~~~~~~~~~~

Merciful God, may Your grace, love, and mercy be all I desire. I pray to embrace Your gift of unmerited favor as my complete sufficiency. O Father, I yield to the Holy Indweller for the perfecting of my weakness to a attain a complete blessed *shalom*. Amen.

DAY 38

*For God gave us a spirit not of fear but of power
and love and self-control.*

—2 Timothy 1:7 ESV

~ ~ ~ ~ ~ ~ ~ ~ ~ ~ ~ ~ ~ ~

*A*s a biblical counselor, I speak to many who struggle with the invasion of fearful thoughts. I refer to these thoughts as "intruders," since they are unwelcome reminders of what shakes us to our core, causing us to be anxiety-ridden and driven by fear. The output of fearful believing can't coexist with faith-filled receiving, as it blocks our spiritual receptors.

For example, this is the acronym for fear I use often: *False Evidence Appearing Real.* This proves out the plague of worry that our fears are false mental imposters of what possible outcomes may be. The evidence is usually benign in nature so as not to find us guilty as we might already have deemed ourselves. The truth of the appearance of our fear is clouded at best, with a lack of transparency apparent to unveil our angst. And lastly, the reality is usually never the exaggerated state of mind that we have indoctrinated as a defining devastation for the final upshot.

The Holy Spirit dwells inside of us to assist with casting out the voices of doubt, anxiety, and utter dread. You have the capacity to vanquish fear right at its evil root though the internal power of God. With the *agape* love of the Father, you can master the fruit of self-control in tandem with the Spirit's boldness. Your Creator fashioned you to strive with an abundant existence, not a fear-based witness.

Action Step of Faith: With your confidence firm in Christ, you can conquer the dark fears that are confronting your well-being. As fear is a spirit, so is faith. Be a change agent in your prayer life, and believe for prosperity with gracious hope, instead of fanning the flames of trepidation.

~~~~~~~~~~~~~~~

O Lord, my God, help me to lay down my fears at Your footstool so I no longer partner with the accuser of the brethren, who weaves fictitious lies that I tend to believe. Adonai, I pray for Your voice to be the loudest one in order for my heart to perceive Your truth. Lord, may my faith rise above my fear. Amen.

_____
_____
_____
_____
_____
_____
_____
_____
_____
_____
_____
_____
_____
_____
_____
_____
_____
_____
_____
_____

DAY
39

We demolish arguments and every pretension
that sets itself up against the knowledge of God,
and we take captive every thought to make it
obedient to Christ.

—2 Corinthians 10:5 NIV

~~~~~~~~~~~~~~

There is something about a new season that promotes a deep cleaning of dresser drawers, wardrobes, and cluttered spaces. I relish the time to reminisce over old memories attached to these precious items that bring warmth to my soul. This would include my grandmother's brooch and my grandfather's wallet, with his last two-dollar bill and his driver's license with photo. At times, it captivates my attention with joyful tears for those "days gone by" which pull upon my heartstrings.

What happens when we hold on to negative items in the cluttered closets of our minds and hearts? The apostle Paul reminds us that we are to exercise control as we proceed with a clean sweep of junk-filled musings. We are to take inventory as we confront every disabling mindset and turn them over to the dumpster that God levies at the foot of the cross. In Christ, we begin to restrain the response to the garbage-heaped conversation that tries to empty its pretenses back into our minds.

Are you able to sift the unwanted, shackled accusations through the mighty hands of Jesus? You can live a life aware of what you're intellectually processing, coinciding with your spiritual behavior. The adversary will try to provoke your memory of old mistakes from the past. Remember, Jesus already threw out the trash when you invited Him to sanitize the interior space of your former self. Garbage in, garbage out! God above you, Jesus next to you, the Holy Spirit within you—and the muck remains in the trash!

Action Step of Faith: When was the last time you needed a "spring cleaning" of your mind? Do you struggle with negative thoughts from the past, or even the present? Be obedient to place those unwanted and uninvited squatters of evil mindsets at the holy door, as you escort them to the curb!

~~~~~~~~~~~~~

Lord Jesus, I pray that You remove any thoughts that are ungodly and unhealthy from my perception. Help me to discern Your words of truth over the enemy's smug reminders of my wicked past. Jesus, I declare that my past has been redeemed at Calvary's cross, and I surrender my life, which has been cleansed by Your precious blood. Amen.

_____
_____
_____
_____
_____
_____
_____
_____
_____
_____
_____
_____
_____
_____
_____
_____
_____
_____
_____
_____

DAY 40

This is My command: be strong and courageous.
Never be afraid or discouraged because I am
your God, the Eternal One, and I will remain
with you wherever you go.

—Joshua 1:9 VOICE

~~~~~~~~~~~~~~

There's nothing like a good old-fashioned fall carnival, with the sounds of laughter, the smells of popcorn, and the rides that give you thrills and chills. Personally, I am not much for the enormous roller coasters, but I have found entertainment in the funhouses. Especially the ones that have all those mirrors that change appearance and distort your shape. (That can be scary all on its own!) Sometimes your reflection can be unrecognizable, but thankfully it's only a manipulation of reality.

I believe depression is capable of the same misrepresentation. When we remain rooted in God's strength and courageous spirit, we don't lose hope, but we gain trust steeped in faith. Depression is hope deferred, which has the ability to twist our situations into a warped sense of continual sadness. This unrelenting detriment tends to result in a palpable decline relationally with Jesus, as His presence atmospherically fades. God provides His blessed assurance, plus the unending empowerment of His commissioned strength to reshape our deepest, despondent hearts.

Is depression your counterpart in this season of life? Perhaps it's time to see with the clarity of your "soul" mirror the true reflection of what God sees when He gazes upon you, His child. Jesus' desire for you is to embrace your life free from fear and discouragement, with Your holy Helper guiding the way. God doesn't just suggest courage to be your standpoint, but He decrees it through His promise of procurement by His Word. Our Lord desires that your strength drenched with joy be found when you surrender your troubled heart into His loving arms.

Action Step of Faith: Today, instead of being isolated and low-spirited, be held by the Spirit of the Living God! Begin to disarm your graveclothes as Jesus places His robe of righteousness upon you. See yourself in the mirror of truth in opposition to the false image that is not inherent of God.

~~~~~~~~~~~~~

El Roi, the God who sees me, I pray to envision my life free from depression, oppression, and any demeaning thoughts. Lord, I place my life at in Your capable hands to remove these strongholds of my mind. Let it be broken and bound in Your mighty name, replaced by Your unspeakable joy and unending love! Amen.

**IF you struggle with any suicidal thoughts and ideations, please call 911 or go to the nearest emergency room for observation. God loves you and desires for you to be made whole, and that sometimes requires medical intervention. A cry for help is a sign of strength! May God go before you!

_____
_____
_____
_____
_____
_____
_____
_____
_____
_____
_____
_____
_____
_____
_____
_____

DAY
41

*"For I know what I have planned for you," says
the LORD. "I have plans to prosper you, not to
harm you. I have plans to give you a future
filled with hope."*

—Jeremiah 29:11 NET

*H*ave you ever glanced at your agenda book and noticed
that a large number of your appointments have resulted
in whiteouts and turnabouts! For some reason, your imminent
appointments just didn't appear to be preordained in the season
of your timetable. I ponder the old adage, "We make plans, and
God laughs!" Sometimes I can hear Him internally chuckling at
my good intentions, as His plans are better destined on my behalf.

God's architecture for His children is drawn up as a blueprint
for our human structures. His ultimate plan is to reconcile and
save us all, without a single exception. The psalmist states in Psalm
57:2, *"I cry out to God Most High, to God who fulfills his purpose for
me"* (ESV). When we offer ourselves to the Lord, we trust His justi-
fication to completion, and He will fulfill the promise of our hope-
filled future. Notwithstanding, He needs our cooperation to cancel
calendared events to allow space for the divine appointments that
lead to prosperity, providence, and God-ordained possibilities.

Have you endured disappointment and frustration waiting
on God's objective while you continue to thrust your own docket
forward? Waiting on God requires discipline and patience, which
is an attainment of ripe holy fruit.

A relationship that is grounded in prayer will enable the
capacity to discern your master plan constructed by the "Author and
Perfecter" of your faith. Abraham Lincoln is quoted as saying, "Good
things come to those who wait." I would add that when those good
things come from our Lord and Savior, the wait is but a joy!

Action Step of Faith: Do you notice a pattern of making plans, changing them, canceling, and restarting again in your schedule? Take account of why you either don't follow through or whose strategic directive you are leaning on. Begin to become intently aware of the Spirit's lead and less of your own. Notice the difference, and journal a potential new outcome.

~ ~ ~ ~ ~ ~ ~ ~ ~ ~ ~ ~ ~

God of Unending Supply, help me to surrender my ways and wants to You as I submit to Your lead. Lord Jesus, I desire to yield to You for daily wisdom, guidance, and enlightenment to reach my ultimate destiny. Amen.

DAY
42

And my God will supply every need of yours
according to his riches in glory in Christ Jesus.
—Philippians 4:9 ESV

~~~~~~~~~~~~~~

Throughout my life, as an Eastern seaboard resident, we have had our fair share of damaging storms, downed trees, and flooding waters. I am forever grateful during those difficult times to have my electricity eventually restored. Sometimes we take for granted our power supply, especially when we lose it amid a momentary outage.

God's supply is always sufficient and generous to those who take heed of His goodness. Our true "needs" pale in comparison to our wants and desires. His riches are not provided for earthly wealth, but for a Kingdom vision resourced through Christ. As a new creature in Christ, you will never lack since your Provider is the supplier of all you will ever require. Somebody, shout "amen!" Even when we have disconnected our plug of faith, God doesn't move—we do.

Are you still connected to Jesus as a life source for all your essential needs? The psalmist tells us that the Lord is our Shepherd; we shall not want (Psalm 23:1). Jesus, as the Great Shepherd, cares for you as His precious lamb, even if you have gone astray. He continues to be your Guide home, as you rejoin the fold of the Lord. God's consecrated power-station will keep the lights on awaiting your arrival!

Action Step of Faith: Has your light gone out because of a recent storm of life or a wreckage of fate? Plug back into your relationship with Jesus Christ as you reconnect at the altar of grace. He loves you and awaits your return to Him with your repentance overflowing to revival.

~~~~~~~~~~~~~~

God of Grace, I thank You that all that I need Your hand hath provided, all the days of my life. I pray to take stock of my supply and posture with gratitude for all that You so graciously pour out over me. Amen.

DAY 43

And we know that in all things God works for
the good of those who love him, who have been
called according to his purpose.
—Romans 8:28 NIV

~~~~~~~~~~~~~~

I can recall back in the "single mom" days, putting together items such as a new gas barbecue. This was very courageous on my part, but I was intent on being able to construct this erector set project nevertheless. I carefully opened the directions, placed all the hardware out, and then the larger pieces of this tremendous endeavor. Long story short, I did finally BBQ burgers that night, but I also had some leftover nuts and bolts, perhaps for my "badge of honor"! However, all the pieces and parts came together for a successful outcome with the deliberate purpose for its inception.

I believe the same is true for the children of God. In our genesis, we were fashioned for a specific purpose as God weaves everything together for good for those who believe in Him. During the course of our stay on earth, we will all endure hardships, long-suffering, sickness, mourning, and many other states of existence. But we will also join those encounters with joy, love, fellowship, peace, and countless definitions of our pleasurable human experiences as sojourners. God will place all these things together to draw us closer, to beget our conformity in Christ, to bear ripe fruit, and ultimately to attain glorification.

How is God working all things together in your life? Can you notice all the fibers and threads of your chronicle entwining a beautiful tapestry of obedience to offer to Christ? Consider your life experiences, whether pleasing or not, and how they have shaped your narrative. God desires to qualify your story for His glory, so as to advance the Kingdom by collaborating all your beautiful strands.

Action Step of Faith: Meditate on your life's benchmarks, and then go back to connect the dots of your arrival. Take account of where you are now, as it is not where you once were, and the future is a blank canvas awaiting your pen. Seek the Holy Spirit's counsel as He waits in that secret place of prayer for you.

~~~~~~~~~~~~~

Lord Jesus, I am so blessed that You love me completely. Prayerfully, I ask You to take my ugly and sinful situations with an inclination to fashion a beautiful, useful creation wanting to honor You each and every day. Amen.

Let us then with confidence draw near to the
throne of grace, that we may receive mercy and
find grace to help in time of need.
—Hebrews 4:16 ESV

*T*hank goodness that I don't have a multitude of memories of entering the dreaded principal's office back in my grade school career, but I have tracked some miles on my children's behalf. I can remember feeling like somewhere along the line, I must have failed in my parental skills, and I usually approached the situation with guilt, infused with anger, and dripping with disappointment. Somehow, the issues that brought tissues worked themselves out with consequences my children needed to own. But I felt laden with self-doubt, as a veiled insecurity loomed over my heart yearning for clarity.

Jesus tells us to approach His altar of grace with confidence as His children. Even as we made erroneous blunders before knowing Christ as our Savior, we continue to slip as fallen, broken people. The difference is the reception of grace and mercy, knowing that God abounds in us especially in our darkest times of need. Jesus shines the light of love into our futile hike of worthlessness, our trails of errors, and our pathways of deceptive thoughts.

You don't have to fear God, as if you are on the walk of shame to the principal's office, but you can revere Him honorably as you enter the throne room of His grace. You can draw near to God today through the confidence in Christ that resonates in your posture of genuine adoration. Jesus, who sits at the right hand of the Father, graciously dispenses help to you and me, as we require forgiveness and strength only found by His hand. If you have made a mess of things, whether past or present, trust that Christ holds your future as you surrender your former self to Him. Only God can make you worthy, only God can make you righteous, only God can forgive your sins, child, only God!

Action Step of Faith: Are you ready to take on the new mind of Christ and lose the negative thoughts of the past? Begin today by being cognizant of the "good things" in your life as you count every silver lining even on the darkest of clouds.

~~~~~~~~~~~~~~

Gracious God, I pray to lay down every thought that is not of You as I embrace Your mercies, which are new each day. Lord, help me to secure my confidence in You as I pursue a deeper relationship captured in the throne room of Your unending love. Amen.

_____

_____

_____

_____

_____

_____

_____

_____

_____

_____

_____

_____

_____

_____

_____

_____

_____

_____

_____

_____

DAY 45

Forget the former things; do not dwell on the past. See, I am doing a new thing! Now it springs up; do you not perceive it? I am making a way in the wilderness and streams in the wasteland.

—Isaiah 43:18–19 NIV

~~~~~~~~~~~~

*A*s you have traversed to the midway point of this devotional book, has your former self decreased as your new self in Christ increased? Do you notice the ability to perceive past issues from a smaller picture as opposed to a "larger-than-life mural" of unprofitable reminders? When we can gaze upon our past—the good, bad, and ugly—with more joy than tears, we have made major strides. Our past can assist in shaping our present-day positions, but it will redefine our future navigation.

Isaiah illumines the former things as the deliverance from Egypt, wading in the parting of the Red Sea waters, the drowning of Pharaoh's armies, and the overthrow of his kingship. But yet greater things are to come. We, too, recount with a posture of thankfulness and praise all to the glory of God, but not to dwell immovable in past recall. God has so much in store for His children so they can achieve and experience abundance in a life lived for Christ. Jesus desires to do new things in our lives, but we must look forward and not backward to gain a true perception for a holy consummation.

Are you where you yearn to be, and if not, can you notice that you are not where you used to dwell? What do you need to acknowledge, change, give up, or let loose of in order to move to the next plateau? The Lord is making clear a pathway! You might need to take a walk in a wilderness or splash through a stream in the desert of life to achieve it.

Action Step of Faith: God is on your side and is a devoted cheerleader in this life. Invite Jesus to create a plan to move your life forward. He desires to clear the cobwebs off your dreams, as your aspirations meet His will for a victorious life well-lived.

~~~~~~~~~~~~~~

Loving Lord, help me to tarry for Your perfect plan, and understand that my past mistakes are the "bones" of positive formation for my future. I pray to see through Your holy lens the narrow path I must continue to travel so I can reach the "brass ring" of Heaven. Amen.

_____
_____
_____
_____
_____
_____
_____
_____
_____
_____
_____
_____
_____
_____
_____
_____
_____
_____
_____
_____

DAY 46

Consider it pure joy, my brothers and sisters,
whenever you face trials of many kinds, because
you know that the testing of your faith produces
perseverance. Let perseverance finish its work
so that you may be mature and complete, not
lacking anything.

—James 1:2–4 NIV

~~~~~~~~~~~~

We all tend to have our own configured bedtime routines. I might spend time reading a book or in prayer, and then the "counting" begins. I take account of my morning agenda before my head actually lands quietly on my pillow. I don't count sheep; I count appointments, deadlines, and emails to return, which defers my sleep. We should all count our blessings regardless of experiencing an abridged season chock-full of exhortation.

James, who was the brother of Jesus, reminds us that our trials also double as our "tests." As Jesus was tested in the wilderness, as believers, we are also placed on trial to procure a judgment evidencing the steadfastness of our faith. The outcome of a steadfast conviction in Christ will perfect our growth in holiness and trust, no matter the verdict of the adversary. Jesus is our Advocate before the Father, and by His spilled blood on the cross, we are found "forgiven."

What are you counting today that might keep you up all night? Are the trials, afflictions, addictions, and tests of this life more than you can endure? There is a Savior who wants to take your burden but also help you strengthen your faith walk in spite of it! The God who tarries in the valley of your situations will also usher you to the mountaintop of endurance, empowerment, and an equipping rescue.

Action Step of Faith: Journal the most difficult tribulations in your life. As you pray, with radical faith, begin to watch God move! Only He can break down the walls and change the atmosphere of situations in the forefront of your heart. God changes us, while in retrospect, "we" are the ultimate test.

〰〰〰〰〰〰

Father God, help me to count it all joy, no matter the trial or test occurring in my life. Lord, prayerfully transform me in the midst of them so I can grow in Your garden of wisdom, discernment, and tenacity of faith. Amen.

_____
_____
_____
_____
_____
_____
_____
_____
_____
_____
_____
_____
_____
_____
_____
_____
_____
_____
_____
_____
_____
_____

DAY 47

*Therefore, take up the whole armor of God,
that you may be able to withstand in the evil
day, and having done all, to stand firm.*
— Ephesians 6:13 ESV

- - - - - - - - - - - -

O ur heroes in the armed forces never enter a battlefield unprepared or ill-equipped. These "called" brothers and sisters engage in many months of boundless training that propels their minds, bodies, and spirits to the outermost realm. Our soldiers also receive an arsenal of equipment, weapons for warfare, and uniform garments representing honor epitomized by bravery.

As soldiers for Christ, we, too, engage in spiritual combat on a daily basis. There is the visible reality that exists in knowing spiritual forces that are evil in nature are no match for our great, almighty God. We, too, as entering the battleground, hold fast the front line against the adversary's charge upon us, our family, and our way of Christian living. But God has provided a "complete" armor from our crown to our toes, consisting of the following spiritual resources: a belt for truth, a breastplate of righteousness, shoes girded in peace, the shield of faith, the helmet of our salvation, and the sword of the Spirit. The army of Christ has been given enough holy ammunition to stand firm when the enemy comes to battle for your soul.

When was the last attack, and what was your ability to remain standing? Are you spiritually suited up daily so you may withstand the enemy in faith and not retreat in fear? God has provided to you, in your rebirth, His Spirit, which remains your partner in all that you battle. The activation of your armor, however, is rooted in a constant posture of prayer and executed with biblical alertness. The Word of God is to be wielded like a sharp two-edged sword, in the mighty power of His Holy Spirit (Hebrews 4:12). Child of God, in this hour, suit up, bow down, and stand firm!

Action Step of Faith: Are you able to remain strong in the Lord or are you prone to lift a white flag of surrender to the schemes of the evil one? Be alert when spiritual warfare begins to capture your heart. Put on the armor of the Lord and watch the Holy Spirit intercede on your behalf.

~~~~~~~~~~~~~~

Jehovah Nissi, You alone are my Protector when I am trapped and overcome with the heaviness of my plights. Lord, I beseech You to gird me in spiritual armor so I will not be defeated by worldly or demonic warfare, but found triumphant through my heart of worship unto You. Amen.

_____
_____
_____
_____
_____
_____
_____
_____
_____
_____
_____
_____
_____
_____
_____
_____
_____
_____
_____

DAY 48

But by the grace of God I am what I am, and His grace toward me did not prove vain; but I labored even more than all of them, yet not I, but the grace of God with me.
— 1 Corinthians 15:10 NASB

There was an old philosopher who was known for saying, "I yam what I yam, and that's all that I yam!" Basically, our friend Popeye was stating that all he was, essentially, was all that he was. I would have to agree, since he was a one-dimensional cartoon with a challenging mode of vocal expression. But this insightful declaration is a placeholder to insert the intention for "that" to be defined as the amazing grace of God.

The apostle Paul is exhorting in this prolific verse that all that we are is encapsulated by the grace of God blanketed over our lives. Paul took account that his conversion from a "persecutor" to an "apostle" was a wholly undeserved gift from the hand of the Lord. God's grace upon his life and ministry was not a road to passivity, but to Kingdom productivity infused with Holy Spirit-filled power. *"Each of you should use whatever gift you have received to serve others, as faithful stewards of God's grace in its various forms"* (1 Peter 4:10 NIV).

This is true for us, the blood-purchased believers in Christ! All that you are is foundational through your Savior by the unmerited favor that seals you as His own. No word and deed are to be considered an act of vanity, but of a reconciled faith yielded with submissive love. Today, you are tasked to be a laborer in the "fields of grace" alongside those who are just gleaning the wheat of seeking Jesus.

Action Step of Faith: What is your perception of your conversion trail? Have you ever attempted to connect the breadcrumbs that you might have left behind as you migrated forward in a newly revealed walk of faith? Take notice and account for the prevenient grace, the grace that wooed you to Christ, that carried you along a pathway of redemption.

~~~~~~~~~~~~~~

Dear Jesus, I pray for a holy nudge of awareness to be eternally thankful for Your spiritual gifts of blessing. Lord, help me never to become complacent or lethargic as Your ambassador in the presence of those who so desperately hunger and thirst for Your mercy and grace! Amen.

_____
_____
_____
_____
_____
_____
_____
_____
_____
_____
_____
_____
_____
_____
_____
_____
_____
_____
_____

DAY 49

God did this so that, by two unchangeable things in which it is impossible for God to lie, we who have fled to take hold of the hope set before us may be greatly encouraged. We have this hope as an anchor for the soul, firm and secure. It enters the inner sanctuary behind the curtain.

—Hebrews 6:18–19 NIV

*A*n anchor is a device designed to connect a vessel to the bed or surface of a body of water to prevent the craft from drifting due to wind or currents. This word is derived from the Greek word *agkura*, which also means "to stay or to safeguard"! The anchor is symbolic of hope, steadfastness, peace, and composure. The anchored cross, or mariner's cross, is also one of the earliest trademarks in Christianity. It is shaped like a plus sign with anchorlike protrusions at the end of each arm, hence the name.

In Christ, we need to fasten ourselves as a "vessel," so that when the storms of life blow in, we can remain firmly secure when rocked by the waves of chaos, confusion, ungodly doctrine, and calamity. Our blessed assurance can experience maximum buoyancy sailing on His ship of truth, forgiveness, and grace. God's promises and purpose are His unchangeable oath to those who share a personal kinship. The Christian hope is established in the personhood and saving work only to be found in Christ.

What is your faith anchored in these days? Is it an anchor rooted in Christ, with stability, steadfastness, and firm standing? Or is it a latch that hooks on to anything that is traveling too closely by you that might keep you stuck in your rut? Make Christ the anchor to your soul today so you will never drift away! An acronym for *HOPE* is this: *H*—hold firmly onto your faith to remain eternally secure; *O*—only find your trust in God alone; *P*—pray without ceasing as the daily meditation of your heart; *E*—every day nourish your soul with the living Word of God.

Action Step of Faith: Be mindful of the deep waters in which you swim, and that your life preserver should always be clothed in Christ. Anything else will just deflate it, when the strong wind and waves come crashing down.

~ ~ ~ ~ ~ ~ ~ ~ ~ ~ ~ ~ ~ ~ ~

Heavenly Lord, I pray to be aware of whom I anchor my soul to in the treacherous waters of life. Father, help me always to find my way back to the shoreline of Your heart and the recognition of Your truth. Amen.

_____

_____

_____

_____

_____

_____

_____

_____

_____

_____

_____

_____

_____

_____

_____

_____

_____

_____

_____

DAY 50

*"The L*ORD *will fight for you, while you keep silent."*

—Exodus 14:14 NASB

*T*here was a time when I enjoyed scary movies, but truth be told, I don't anymore. I would watch between my sweaty fingers that partially covered my eyes as my stomach knotted with suspense. That doesn't sound very appealing, but I enjoyed the adrenaline rush a long time ago. Today, I do not find any pleasure in fearful situations, not onscreen, and especially not in real time! We all have experienced terrifying circumstances that resulted in a phone ringing either way too early in the morning or far too late at night. My faith in Christ alone has been my only way to prevail peacefully when life is unequivocally not!

Moses led the Israelites out of Egypt as Pharaoh and his fleet of chariots were marching after their hurried footsteps to the Red Sea. Moses told them to fear not and to stand firm, as they sought the salvation of the Lord. He also declared that after all the plagues, battle forces, and evil they endured, their God would deliver them as they kept their faith moving forward. Yet, He coveted a postured stance of quieted confidence and assured trust from His people. Just as these forefathers of ours did, let's stop to realize that our greatest challenges and most fear-filled moments are opportunities for the Lord to expand our faith.

What holds you captive in fear and worry these days? The Lord sees us in our times of greatest need as He desires for us to stand still before Him, and not run away. When you are surrounded on all sides, trust in the Lord's faithful promises to fight on your behalf. Gather your rest time in stillness, at the gracious hand of your Father, who holds you securely in the shelter of His love.

Action Step of Faith: Identify your fear and worry by name. So often we embrace it as a blanket that was never meant to cover our "being"! Cast it into the fire, and place the garments of praise over you, which will provide the release of the spirit of heaviness to be forever removed.

~ ~ ~ ~ ~ ~ ~ ~ ~ ~ ~ ~ ~ ~ ~

Jesus, Love of my Soul, guard my life by day and by night as You command Your angels to watch over me. I pray to fear less while trusting You more, so I may strive to thrive in confidence, bound to my providential Creator. Amen.

_____

_____

_____

_____

_____

_____

_____

_____

_____

_____

_____

_____

_____

_____

_____

_____

_____

_____

_____

_____

_____

You keep track of all my sorrows. You have collected all my tears in your bottle. You have recorded each one in your book.
—Psalm 56:8 NLT

*M*any of us can stake a claim to shedding numerous tears, whether it be on the bathroom floor, on the pounded pavements, or at a dimly lit church altar. Spanning troubled situations, difficult health diagnoses, and painful relational issues, I have personally filled many jars of these salt-filled droplets of liquid emotion. Isn't a reassuring fact that God places all of our accountable tears in His holy jar of redemption?

The psalmist's lament is heartfelt, when he states that even in the midst of his enemies' schemes, God's love is forever faithful. Jesus keeps a viable record of the tears of His faithful ones as He is not an absentee parent. He cares for the brokenness of our hearts, as He desires to reinstate us fully by wholeness and recompense founded only by our trust in Him.

Have you ever endured a life phase that effectuated a time to weep? Even to the extent of puffy, reddened eye sockets so that you could barely open them? God was there with you in those blurry moments of extreme sorrow and anguish. While He interceded for each droplet, He collected them in His jar, and He counted them, so His healing could regenerate your heart.

Action Step of Faith: You might not have ever thought to count your tears, but your Savior has already covered that for you. Give God the glory, even in strife, as you run the course of long-suffering. He has already formulated a pathway to your unique resolution of joy. "Weeping may last for the night, but a shout of joy comes in the morning" (Psalm 30:5 NASB).

~~~~~~~~~~~~~~

Jesus, my Great Redeemer, thank You for loving me enough to count every hair upon my head and all the tears I have ever shed. Lord, I pray to have gratitude for Your master plan, even in the pain, as I know that the dawn will be ever so near in my midst. Amen.

_____
_____
_____
_____
_____
_____
_____
_____
_____
_____
_____
_____
_____
_____
_____
_____
_____
_____
_____
_____

But if we freely admit our sins when his light
uncovers them, he will be faithful to forgive
us every time. God is just to forgive us our
sins because of Christ, and he will continue
to cleanse us from all unrighteousness. 1
John 1:9 TPT

~~~~~~~~~~~~

*T*he act of forgiveness is not always an easy and natural process, especially when you have been the recipient of deep
verbal cuts and spiritual bruises. Just as I have sinned in the darkness of my fleshly proclivities, Jesus endeavors to shine His light
to uncover the truth of my wrongdoing, incorrect actions, and
unrighteous attitudes. But God doesn't just unmask it; He offers
full remission through our spoken word of confession as we are
cleansed by His love.

When we profess by our mouths to be forgiven, Jesus is faithful to offer just that…forgiveness. Our covenant with the Lord
tasks the believer to forgive others as Christ has forgiven us. It
sounds theologically correct as we understand the principle, but
we struggle with the concept of holiness. Only through our daily
divine interactions with God will the spiritual equipping mold us
with the supernatural capacity to impart mercy and grace to others.

Do you struggle with forgiving others, while asking God for
forgiveness for yourself? The ability to be symbiotic in both disciplines is what releases you from the bondage of unforgiveness.
Compare it to taking a sip of poison while waiting for another to
die. In reality, you are the one that is withering from the inside out!
Forgiveness is a holy habit that is a genuine catalyst to a manifestation of submission to first Christ, and then others.

Action Step of Faith: Each day is an opportunity for confession with holy pardon. Go before the Lord and invite Him into the struggle of your chains of unforgiveness. Keep account of each shackle the Lord has loosed on your behalf! Practice makes perfect, and one day you will receive glorified perfection in eternity!

~~~~~~~~~~~~~~

Father God, I pray to relinquish my heart and mind bound up in shackles of anger, mercilessness, bitterness, and rage. Lord, in Your mercy, edify me with Your tenets of love, wrapped in forgiveness, as You unlock my chains of pain. Amen.

DAY
53

"Because of God's tender mercy, the morning light from heaven is about to break upon us, to give light to those who sit in darkness and in the shadow of death, and to guide us to the path of peace."

—Luke 1:78–79 NLT

~~~~~~~~~~~~~

*T*here is something so very hope-inspiring about the beautiful majesty captured in a morning sunrise, in the hues of a golden sun breaking against the gray-toned sky. I seek the promise that is peeking its eye through the clouds as it surrounds the atmosphere in a blanket of peace. The Hebrew word for peace is *shalom*, which is a complete and whole sense of tranquility. The *shalom* of daybreak provides the mastery to sense God's presence as His mercies are newly gifted daily!

As Zechariah was filled with the Holy Spirit, he prophesied the coming of the Messiah, the foretelling of the One who would provide the light in the darkness, even in the shadow of death. In the Sermon on the Mount, Jesus would teach us to strive to be peacemakers, as He would be the model to impart that posture to the world. *"Blessed are the peacemakers, for they will be called children of God"* (Matthew 5:9 NIV).

How would you rate your ability to remain peaceful throughout your day? Peace must first start within us, before we can convey that attribute to another. A dawn experience, wrapped in the tender arms of your Savior, inherently generates the stillness that will capture your day and keep it tranquil. It is a discipline to train yourself to cast all worries, anxiety, and deadlines at the feet of Jesus, so your burdens will be light. Jesus' intention for us was not to live easy, but as saved children, we have a newly formed predisposition to easily live.

Action Step of Faith: Does your morning ritual create a space for God to set your daily tone? Be mindful to make time for Jesus before your feet touch the floor, so He can guide the remainder of your day.

~~~~~~~~~~~~~~

God of peace, I pray each morning to offer You the "first-fruits" of my time daily. Lord Jesus, guide me throughout my day so I can remain cocooned in Your peace, love, mercy, and grace until my head reconnects with my pillow. Amen.

_____

_____

_____

_____

_____

_____

_____

_____

_____

_____

_____

_____

_____

_____

_____

_____

_____

_____

_____

*Then Jesus said to his disciples, "Whoever wants
to be my disciple must deny themselves and take
up their cross and follow me."*
> —Matthew 16:24 NIV

~~~~~~~~~~~~

We are marked by the uniqueness of our individual fingerprints! Each of us strategizes a personal voyage that awaits our lives, which have been designated by God's perfect plan. Following the guidelines of our Spirit-led advisor, we can successfully evidence a well-established witness in the example found only in Christ.

Jesus is transparent as to the actions of His disciples to effectively release themselves from an earthly life. A believer is to deny himself, pick up his cross, and follow after our Lord. The Kingdom sacrifice will be priceless as an eternal promise to those who heed the call. The worldly pleasures, financial gain, or title of power could never match the thought of a forfeited soul.

Can you hear God calling you closer to Him in this hour? Jesus loves you too much to leave you in a pit of darkness, as He desires an authentic relationship with you. Jesus wants to break the power of sin that is active in your life so you can deny yourself, die to self, and live harmoniously in Christ. The suffering you might bear for our Savior will, one glorious day, lead you into triumphant glory.

Action Step of Faith: Take notice of your social circle and your sphere of influence each day. Are you standing in your witness or bending in apprehension? Seek God daily to stand firm with affirmation to lead the way for others to Christ.

~~~~~~~~~~~~~~

Jesus, my Savior, help me to hear Your voice above all the clamor in this culture. I beseech You to help me follow You above all else! Lord, I call upon Your holy name for godly clarity, righteous living, and faith-filled accountability. Amen.

_____

_____

_____

_____

_____

_____

_____

_____

_____

_____

_____

_____

_____

_____

_____

_____

_____

_____

_____

_____

_____

_____

DAY 55

"To proclaim the year of the LORD's favor and the day of vengeance of our God, to comfort all who mourn, and provide for those who grieve in Zion to bestow on them a crown of beauty instead of ashes, the oil of joy instead of mourning, and a garment of praise instead of a spirit of despair. They will be called oaks of righteousness, a planting of the LORD for the display of his splendor."
—Isaiah 61:2–3 NIV

*M*ost of us reach a place in our lives where we have experienced deep and painful loss. Quantifiable sorrow can be experienced when a best friend, family member, beloved fur baby, or child departs from our sight. Typically, what then follows is a season of mourning to properly lament the broken-heartedness of a traumatic absence. The remedy calls for a time of stillness connected to the only genuine Source of comfort, mercy, and peace, Jesus Christ.

The prophet is relaying to the people of God that some will enter into a chasm of time spent in suffering and pain when they sin against their Lord. This, too, is an example of mourning when they experience God's wrath. Only with His mercy and grace, God adorned them with a beautiful crown for their ceremonial ashes. It was customary that they would cover themselves with embers to represent a remorseful, bereaved disposition.

Are you cloaked in soot or sporting a kingly crown? The Lord desires for you to be in possession of the oil of joy instead of sorrow and a garment of praise as the antidote for a spirit of despair. If you are mourning from a departed love relationship with Jesus, release your confession to lift the heaviness of desolation. Your true peace will be sustained even in the midst of dire circumstances only propagated by the hope of heaven.

Action Step of Faith: Unshroud your sadness in exchange for a robe of righteousness. Present your full cup of transgressions at His footstool to receive your provision of His splendor!

~~~~~~~~~~~~~~~

Heavenly Father, guide my path back to You when You stray from the eyes of my heart. I pray to seek You in the driest of deserts and in the deepest of valleys in my life. May I forever seek a crown to cast before Your throne! Amen.

_____
_____
_____
_____
_____
_____
_____
_____
_____
_____
_____
_____
_____
_____
_____
_____
_____
_____
_____
_____
_____
_____
_____
_____
_____

DAY 56

*"But like the Holy One who called you, be holy
yourselves in all your conduct [be set apart from
the world by your godly character and moral
courage]; because it is written, "YOU SHALL BE
HOLY [set apart], FOR I AM HOLY."*
—1 Peter 1:15–16 AMP

~~~~~~~~~~~~

T he Christian lifestyle has a daily call to ward off the tugging
of worldly pulls so we can live freely in the light of love. A
severing of sorts, tasked by the child of God, is to unhinge from
the herd's behavior while demonstrating the character of the Lord.
This is not always easily attained if we are not seeking God daily.
We are held to a higher standard, as we are called to be "holy"
because God is holy.

We can only achieve this level of godly aptitude by divine
intervention since the fall of Adam described in Genesis 3. When
we are born again into a new life in Christ, the Holy Spirit takes up
permanency within our heart, mind, language, and behavior. The
sanctification process begins to form as we are consecrated while
maturing in His grace.

God commands you to be a life celebrated in holiness. That
sounds like an impossible order since Jesus is perfect and humans
are not. Each day surrender your old ways to the Lord as you are
clothed in righteousness. This is the evidence of the work of the
Spirit cleansing us from the inside out as we remain in full cooperation. Walk in your call to dance in His light, as our Father sets
you apart to shine on His behalf.

Action Step of Faith: Attest by your faith to live in the world but not to mirror this world. Be mindful of the choices you make each day to remain set apart for His glory.

~~~~~~~~~~~~~~~

O Lord, help me to remain obedient when the world attempts to pull my strings of morality, character, and right living. Prayerfully, I bow before You to desire Your ways above any other while remaining consecrated to You. Jesus, forgive me when I stray, as the Holy Spirit lovingly lifts me up once again and brings me back home. Amen.

_____
_____
_____
_____
_____
_____
_____
_____
_____
_____
_____
_____
_____
_____
_____
_____
_____
_____
_____
_____
_____
_____

*But as for me, it is good to draw near to God.
I have made the Lord GOD my refuge, that I
may proclaim all Your works.*
—Psalm 73:28 BSB

*H*ave you ever taken notice of what you are attracted to? Let's compare a magnet to a piece of steel for a moment. A substance that encompasses the components for a magnetic field will draw, by a physical force, iron and steel. Yet, if you take your magnet away from the metal and turn it around, it will repel the metal, because it was magnetized by an opposite pole.

Our inherent nature given through Christ should draw us closer, as a magnet is attracted to metal. If we are charged by a repelling force, our spiritual direction will push back. The psalmist declares that it is a "good" thing to draw near to God, as those who deflect in the opposite direction will perish. We can rest assured that by placing our full trust and confidence in Christ alone, we can remain covered under His wings of protection, mercy, and love. Our testimony should be a daily proclamation to the goodness of God and the portion of sufficiency that flows to our souls.

Are you nearing ever so close to Jesus each day? If not, what force outside of your faith is luring you away? God desires an intimate relationship with you, which requires your pressing into Him. If you are not leaning into Jesus daily, what are you being attracted to instead? Be alert and aware that what you gravitate to will eventually stick onto your evidence of your witness and works.

Action Step of Faith: Be mindful that whatever you attach yourself to is never more desirable than the wooing voice of the Holy Spirit! Truth talk for the blood-bought children of God! Your surroundings will expose your inward attractions.

~~~~~~~~~~~~~~

Precious Lord, I pray to bloom where I am planted in Your garden full of grace. May I continually draw ever closer so that I can sense Your breath upon my lifted countenance. Amen.

_____

_____

_____

_____

_____

_____

_____

_____

_____

_____

_____

_____

_____

_____

_____

_____

_____

_____

_____

_____

_____

_____

_____

_____

DAY 58

I have been crucified with Christ. It is no longer I
who live, but Christ who lives in me. And the life
I now live in the flesh I live by faith in the Son of
God, who loved me and gave himself for me.

—Galatians 2:20 ESV

*I*n today's society, surrender is not a popular manifesto regarding sacrificing one's pleasure for a "narrow path" of life. We are bombarded with a multitude of intel propelling us to embrace the lie that the one with the most toys wins! My question is, "Wins what?" Someone once said that I never saw a Hertz towing a U-Haul! The more we yield ourselves to the Father, the less the material, physical, sexual, and manufactured spiritual aspects of this planet will appeal to our carnal human nature.

As a Christian, the crux of our faith is to surrender our flesh daily to gain a holy perspective of dying to our self-serving ways. When we are crucified with Christ, we are a new creation; our sins have been imputed to Jesus, the One who had no sin. That is what I define as the greatest win one could ever strive for in this life, to live fully for Jesus. The act of submitting ourselves daily to God begins the process of destroying selfishness, prideful attitudes, and amorous desires. We learn the power to say "no" to sinful behavior and "yes" as a reverential response to the deep love we have for Christ.

Have you given your life to Christ so He may reside in your heart and so that you can be crucified with Him? Perhaps your answer might be "yes," or "no," or "that was a long time ago"! In this moment, invite Jesus to be the Lord of your life, as we are all sinners in need of a Savior. Confess before Him, by your mouth, your sins, as you cannot save yourself. Declare that Jesus is Lord and believe in your heart that God raised Him from the dead. For it is with your heart that you believe and are justified, and it is by your tongue that you profess your faith and are saved. When you accept Christ into your heart, He welcomes you into the adopted family of His heavenly Kingdom.

Action Step of Faith: If this is the first time you have accepted Christ into your life, let me be the first to say, "Welcome to the family!" Find a Bible-believing church and gift yourself a Bible! If there have been countless number of times you've reaffirmed your faith, track where you fall off! All you need to do is call upon the name of Jesus, and He will lift you up again, as He loves you and He desires to spend eternity with you.

Father God, I confess when I fall short of Your glory, but I am a sinner saved by my Savior as I continually pursue You every day, forevermore. Holy Spirit, guide my path daily so that I remain robed with Your righteousness, blessed by Your grace, and clothed in Christ. Amen.

DAY
59

In my distress I called to the LORD, and he answered me. Deliver me, O LORD, from lying lips, from a deceitful tongue.

—Psalm 120:1–2 ESV

~~~~~~~~~~~~

*E*very now and then, I will look up information on my devices whereby the search engine provides either unwelcome information or unsolicited advice. Over the years, so many good-intentioned individuals have shared their thoughts, including unrequested comments, character assassinations, and personal criticisms. For some reason, the downloads of negativity always seem to remain in my personal files in comparison to the deleted positive remarks.

Human nature sets us up for an experiential exchange of distress, often at the lashing tongue of another. When we prayerfully call upon the name of the Lord, He answers us, as the psalmist records in this lament of deliverance. God desires His children to sojourn encouraged in the truth of His promises and in opposition to the commentary of worldly opinions. Those with lying lips can only benefit by the power of their deceit if we shift into their corners.

Why do we at times feed their lies and starve our truths? Believe what the Lord has written in His countless "I Am" statements about you! Where did you start investing in a distorted image of who you are? In your saved identity, release the past misnomers that were placed upon you while you were acquiring the mind of Christ. Be attentive, not only regarding "who" you are, but "whose" you belong to, as a wanted and cherished child of the King. "I am the apple of your eye; hide me in the shadow of your wings" (see Psalm 17:8).

Action Step of Faith: Take stock of what you believe about yourself. If you have bought the deceptive downloads from your past, it's time to wash your intel clean! Journal the promises of God; meditate on His ever-flowing stream of love as your pain recedes.

~~~~~~~~~~~~~~

Dear Jesus, I pray to intertwine my heartstrings to Yours as I disconnect the choking vines from my past. Help me to recognize myself the way Your eyes embrace me, with a precious *agape* expression. Amen.

_____
_____
_____
_____
_____
_____
_____
_____
_____
_____
_____
_____
_____
_____
_____
_____
_____
_____
_____
_____
_____
_____

The Spirit of God, who raised Jesus from the dead, lives in you. And just as God raised Christ Jesus from the dead, he will give life to your mortal bodies by this same Spirit living within you.

—Romans 8:11 NLT

*H*ave you ever walked into a darkened room and attempted to switch on the lamp, only to discover it's unplugged? Until you can finally blaze a trail to the outlet, in the darkness you remain! The only way to be spiritually charged is to be plugged in to the Spirit of perpetual life and light. An unattached plug cannot receive energy to be useful for anything, just as an unsaved person does not have the strength or power autonomously to receive the promise of salvation.

Jesus has given to us the Spirit that resurrected Him to life, which now indwells us. Our blessed assurance is crested in the hope of the risen Christ, who one day will elevate us to a life covenanted in eternity. This holy source is only available through the conduit of the Spirit. Jesus is the only power source that connects our resources of knowledge, gifts, and graces to exceed our earthly comprehension, aptitude, and expectation.

Do you seek to know more about God's power? It is through the "transformed life" where the holy light switch can endeavor an enduring power surge. As you experience your new life in Christ, cleave to the inner strength that resides within you, as this is the same power that raised Christ from the dead. Meditate on that thought, as it is a glorious mystery to our finite minds.

Action Step of Faith: Partner in cooperation with the indwelling Spirit to do the embedded work for the Kingdom of God. Walk in your authority as a believer to stand and resist all evil, as the enemy will flee by the spoken name and words of Jesus Christ (James 4:7).

~~~~~~~~~~~~~~~

Glorious God, help me to walk in my authority and strength found in You alone, who lives in me. I yearn to be molded into a vessel of honor as I stand firmly on Your Word. Let me be found fully alive and freely forgiven, as I once was dead in my sin and my unregenerate spirit, but now I am reborn into the likeness of Christ. Amen.

"A Redeemed Life" in Christ in the Next 30 Days

DAY 61

Do everything without complaining and argu-
ing, so that no one can criticize you. Live clean,
innocent lives as children of God, shining like
bright lights in a world full of crooked and per-
verse people. Hold firmly to the word of life;
then, on the day of Christ's return, I will be
proud that I did not run the race in vain and
that my work was not useless.
—Philippians 2:14–16 NLT

A magnifying glass will bring into focus everything that can't be seen by the natural eye. Typically, the purpose of such a lens is to expose the finely detailed items that might be missed otherwise. Living in our culture, I have felt the pressured lens of objectivity, twisted skepticism, and exhaustive criticism magnified while abiding in Christ Jesus. Each day can compare to a battleground of thoughts, emotions, and actions, but graciously captured by our faithful God, who goes before us.

The apostle Paul was reminding the church at Philippi to be steadfast as they walked out, while working out, their salvation. His utmost concern was that they grasped tightly onto the Word of Life as they exemplified it by their obedient behavior privately as well as publicly. They were tasked to be bright carriers of God's light, just as we are to do the same in our confused and crooked world.

Are you running the race of endurance for the Lord, or have you left to sit on the sidelines? This is your opportunity to gather yourself, dust off the world, and put on the robe of righteousness that the Lord fashioned for His redeemed child. Spend time with others whose lights are brightly shining for Jesus so you, too, can catch on "revival" fire again.

Action Step of Faith: Seek to be aware of your holy temperature. If you are cold, it's time to return to God with a heart rendered fully open. If you are burning hot with fervor for revival, seek the lost who need to be in the light. But if you are lukewarm, run to the altar of repentance as you encounter the Lord in a transformative way! Burn deeply again for Christ.

~~~~~~~~~~~~~~

Loving Lord, help me to stand firmly with a burning passion to evidence my redeemed faith with others who have fallen off the holy trail. Father, I pray to be a useful soldier in Your army to advance the Kingdom of God for Your unending glory. Amen.

*Don't use foul or abusive language. Let every-
thing you say be good and helpful, so that your
words will be an encouragement to those who
hear them.*

—Ephesians 4:29 NLT

~~~~~~~~~~~~

*T*he tongue can be deemed the most powerful part of our
human body. It also has the propensity to be quite lethal,
especially when targeted at another's sense of self-confidence,
self-esteem, and mental stability. Perhaps it is the most dangerous ammunition in one's personal arsenal. Thoughts of schoolyard
bullies, gossiping jeers as you depart the office breakroom, or vile
obscenities that have been regurgitated in marital disputes qualify
as weapons of mass destruction to one's serenity.

As a practicing Christian, our language is to be "seasoned
with salt," and please, hold the pepper. The apostle Paul offered
godly practicum to the church at Ephesus, that they were to halt
from using evil speech while exchanging it for uplifting conversation. Other translations use the term *corrupting talk*, which in the
Greek applies to "bad" speech, also synonymous with "rotten" and
"putrid spiritual fruit." Paul explained during the threads of conversation with others that we are be mindful of weaving "in" grace,
while needling "out" unscrupulous chatter.

As God has blessed you with His grace, you are commanded
to extend that same gift to those with whom you interact each
day. How challenging is it for you to extend grace to others who
are not encouraging or kind in their posture of reciprocation?
Leaning into the Holy Spirit's supernatural strength to love those
who might despise you will gird your faith, which has been sealed
by redemption.

Action Step of Faith: Got Jesus? If so, then speak as if He was in the room, or on the phone, or even looking through your text messages. Be accountable to your language to both yourself and others, as sinful talk is a snare to your faith walk.

~~~~~~~~~~~~

Dear Lord, forgive me when my language, attitude, and speech are offensive to Your ears. Jesus, I pray for holy conviction over my tongue, as I extend grace, mercy, and love to all of God's people as You shower Your unmerited favor upon me. Amen.

_____

_____

_____

_____

_____

_____

_____

_____

_____

_____

_____

_____

_____

_____

_____

_____

_____

_____

_____

_____

_____

_____

DAY
63

*All Scripture is inspired by God and is useful
to teach us what is true and to make us realize
what is wrong in our lives. It corrects us when
we are wrong and teaches us to do what is right.
God uses it to prepare and equip his people to do
every good work.*

—2 Timothy 3:16–17 NLT

~~~~~~~~~~~~

*H*ave you ever had to stop and ask for directions? Did you ever receive directional guidance that was confusing, complicated, or just downright incorrect? But did that make you consider the source? At times, we seek enlightenment from those who are not in the know, or those who might mean well, but they send us on a "not-so-joyful" ride. When it comes to understanding your Bible, your first source of revelation should be Jesus Christ.

Our scriptural Word is God-breathed, as it counsels us with holy instruction to manage our lives. Through the lines of verse, we are reproofed, corrected, and shepherded back to the truth of the Lord's original design to conduct our daily business. Studying our Bible regularly enables our own ability to be equipped, empowered, and encouraged to know the difference between sound theology and false doctrine. If you aren't inspirationally informed, you could fall prey to an idolatry conformation.

Is your Bible in sight? The Word should be in your frontal view, so you don't overlook your daily, divine appointment to ascertain God's unveiling discovery. Your Bible is a road map to a lifestyle lived for Christ and preparation to serve His Kingdom.

Action Step of Faith: If you don't have a Bible, get one. If you have a Bible, feed your heart and mind with it daily. Locate a Bible-based church with a pastor who is sound in doctrine that lines up with every jot and tittle of the inspired Word of God. BIBLE: Basic, Instructions, Before, Leaving, Earth.

~~~~~~~~~~~~

Holy Spirit, prayerfully inscribe every syllable and consonant of Scripture on my heart as You fill my mind with Your spoken word. May I be a carrier of the Light of Your Love as Your ambassador of truth to a dark, harsh world. Amen.

DAY 64

*Now the Lord is the Spirit, and where the Spirit
of the Lord is, there is freedom.*
—2 Corinthians 3:17 ESV

~~~~~~~~~~~~

*T*hroughout the Bible, there are many symbolic signs evidenced that illustrate the promises of God's love, peace, and hope. For example, in the Genesis flood narrative, God placed a rainbow in the sky as His covenant promise that He would never again destroy the earth by this means. The symbolic design of the rainbow is one of new hope established by a fresh beginning. The dove has been an iconic symbol of peace, new life, and purity, as well as the sign of the Holy Spirit.

The Spirit that dwells in the heart of a believer brings about a new life, founded in our second birth. The bondages and shackles from the old self are released by the Spirit's power and purity, while the atonement for our iniquities liberates us from slavery to reconciliation. True freedom comes from our salvation only found in Christ, in tandem with the presence of the Holy Ghost.

In your faith journey, have more chains fallen off than have been placed upon you? Jesus Christ is the Keeper of that key to unlock holy emancipation from condemnation, guilt, transgression, death, the old covenant, and the clarity of the Gospel. Living within you is the flow of the Spirit that gives access to the loving presence of God so you can be set free from the strongholds of sin. *"So, if the Son sets you free, you will be free indeed"* (John 8:36).

Action Step of Faith: Seek the advice of the Holy Counselor for conviction to live righteously. Ask God to provide wisdom and discernment, especially over decisions that might be pending in your heart as to whether or not to bring to fruition in this hour. Traverse with the Dove of the Spirit to guide your way for sustainable peace.

~ ~ ~ ~ ~ ~ ~ ~ ~ ~ ~ ~

Dear Lord, thank You for sending Your Spirit to live and dwell within me. Prayerfully I incline my heart to actively abide in You, so I may be more attuned to the Spirit's lead. May I always be found as a useful vessel for God's Kingdom. Amen.

_____
_____
_____
_____
_____
_____
_____
_____
_____
_____
_____
_____
_____
_____
_____
_____
_____
_____
_____
_____

{ DAY 65 }

Yet God has made everything beautiful for its
own time. He has planted eternity in the human
heart, but even so, people cannot see the whole
scope of God's work from beginning to end.
—Ecclesiastes 3:11 NLT

~~~~~~~~~~~~

*I*n the season of winter, nature lies dormant, awaiting the springtime alarm to reawaken unto a new life. The snow-covered grass blanketing the sleeping flowers will once again break ground and expose their beauty. The human heart waits patiently for the glorious seasons of life to pass from one form to another as God fashions us from womb to tomb.

Our own lives mirror that redemptive journey, traveling from one space of time to another, as we traverse closer to triumphant glory. The word *beautiful* in this verse can also be translated to mean "appropriate." As children of God, we don't always understand the higher plan, but it compels us to seek out the ultimate purpose of our existence. We are to trust, by faith, that the Lord will expose knowledge and direct our course by His mighty will. Even though we are not privy to the Master's plan, we can rest assured, in Christ, that we have perfect peace of a promised hope.

Have you ever spent time trying to decipher God's plan for your life? Sometimes the pieces seem to fit with such ease, and I call that the "green light" effect. Yet at other times, it is one red light after another, while you still run the cautionary signs to wait upon the Lord. Can you recognize that the desire to know everything and the limitations of your ability to do so have been ordained by God? Allow the Lord to guide your path, as His timing is always better than our blind ambition.

Action Step of Faith: Where are you in the grand scheme of life? We tend to be either just entering a new season, experiencing our outcome, or waiting for a new door to open. Spend time with Jesus to garner with clarity His goals, combined with the gifts that have already been deposited within you to accomplish your greatest encounter.

~ ~ ~ ~ ~ ~ ~ ~ ~ ~ ~ ~

Heavenly Creator, help me to trust You more with the life You created me to consummate in this fragile jar of clay. I pray to be shaped, kneaded, and formed into the vessel of Your intended design, not the image that continually shatters Your beautiful mold. Amen.

_____

_____

_____

_____

_____

_____

_____

_____

_____

_____

_____

_____

_____

_____

_____

_____

_____

_____

_____

*Do not be slothful in zeal, be fervent in spirit,
serve the Lord. Rejoice in hope, be patient in
tribulation, be constant in prayer.*
—Romans 12:11–12 ESV

~ ~ ~ ~ ~ ~ ~ ~ ~ ~ ~ ~

I enjoy the blessings of devouring the Word of God in its many different forms of translations and languages. Nevertheless, the final extraction is all God-breathed and Spirit-led through the design of the Lord's revelation to His engaged readers. This translation of verse is entitled, "Marks of a True Christian," and it illustrates a holy interpretation of a genuine believer.

The apostle Paul urged the Christian community to endeavor to have a fervor for God, in spirit and in faith. He further decrees three commands that are essential to the emotional and spiritual well-being of the Body of Christ. Our attitudes should adjust to joy as we stand on our promises, grounded in sharing the hope of being united with our Father. When afflictions enter in, remaining aware of the glory to come will promote the empowerment of victory in the troubling and tarrying times. Then, Paul exhorts them to be in a posture of unceasing prayer. Prayer keeps us connected to God through the Holy Spirit, as Jesus sticks closer than a relative.

Does this checklist of commands somewhat parallel your daily target of a godly lifestyle? Can you notice your strengths and deficits with an ability for some tweaking? The more you can master focusing on the expectations of eternity outside of a worldly reality, you can experience heaven on earth. God imparted knowledge through the Bible so evil would be subdued in any form as you claim your victory in Christ. To be abiding prayerfully is also a chief weapon of spiritual warfare. Stand firm in your affirmation as "boots on the ground" in the army of the Most-High King.

Action Step of Faith: Keep praying, practice patience, and exercise your inherent birthright of daily joy. Journal both assets and shortcomings while finding a balance scale for optimum fruit-filled living!

~~~~~~~~~~~~

Gracious God, I pray to grow more fervently in my faith, being joyful in somber times of patience, and pursuing prayer as my earnest conviction. Lord, may Your face shine upon mine so I may understand the "measure of faith" that You have released unto me. Amen.

_____
_____
_____
_____
_____
_____
_____
_____
_____
_____
_____
_____
_____
_____
_____
_____
_____
_____
_____
_____

*O Lord, you are my God. I will exalt You, I
will praise Your name, for You have done won-
derful things; Your counsels of old are faithfulness and truth.*

—Isaiah 25:1 NKJV

*T*here is nothing better than marking exciting events, benchmarks in life, and joyful encounters with the ones whom you
love! What fond memories those times create as a snapshot of a life
well-traveled. Can you see God in those instances, flowing through
the sands of time? He is literally taking notice, with a sacred poise
of praise, as we acknowledge His faithfulness so that we can celebrate our personal repurchase.

Could we ever account for all the blessings that have been
bestowed upon us from our Savior? That would challenge the
impossible task of tallying the stars in the sky and all the grains
of sand on every shoreline. In our lifetime, we could continually
glorify the name of Jesus for all the remarkable acts that bear His
supernatural and divine fingerprints. God is raising up a remnant
who will always extol His mighty name, no matter the trials that
come their way. His promises of steadfastness and truth are our
inheritance once we are adopted into Christ's family.

Have you lifted your hands to the Lord today in great
exhortation with abiding adoration? Every morning as the dawn
breaks free for the sun to rise, let the "Son" arise in your praise.
Commemorate, as you construct an altar by your thanksgiving for
all the Lord has already completed, perhaps ejected, and in His
will, advanced as His sojourning child.

Action Step of Faith: Do you count your blessings or your disappointments? Somedays it might be a combination of both. Engage God intimately as a loving Father who formed good things for your life; cooperate victoriously with His "better" plan.

~~~~~~~~~~~~~

Dear Lord, I pray to give You all the glory, honor, and praise for climbing Calvary's tree so I can now live free. Abba Father, may my worship always be an acceptable offering as a joyful noise in Your ear. Amen.

DAY
68

He has shown you, O mortal, what is good. And what does the LORD require of you? To act justly and to love mercy and to walk humbly with your God.

—Micah 6:8 NIV

~ ~ ~ ~ ~ ~ ~ ~ ~ ~

*C*omprehension was never a gift of ease or a strong suit of mine growing up. To be completely candid, I still have to press in deeply to understand what I read. The Bible can be a challenge for some, as the Scriptures might not flow congruently and transparently for them. However, there are verses that are as direct as the point of an arrowhead. They hit the mark of Christian absolutes as the "marching orders" of how one should conduct themselves on the frontlines in the army of God.

Micah is one of the twelve minor prophets in the Old Testament who often spoke about the judgment and forgiveness of the Lord. In this verse, we are tasked by the unabashed requirements of primary forms of love in action. Clearly, the decree is for His people to do justice, to love kindness, and to walk humbly in faithfulness with our God. When we reciprocate with a likewise response, we are expressing our love for Jesus' redemptive acts. It is only through His righteousness, which has been imputed to us in our new birth, that we can source the ability to follow His lead.

Does the clarity of God's Word come easy to you? We are to read the Bible as if we were digesting a meal. First take a small bite, then chew well on the Word, and finally digest so the Spirit can help you to rest fully satisfied. In the meditation process of our Bible banquet, God can minister to our spirits proper guidance, instruction, and holy education for our true illumination. Humility should be the road we travel, while paved with mercy, and undergirded by imparting justice wherever the Great Commission sends us.

Action Step of Faith: Create a space for your actions to be reflective of the Lord's requirements in Micah 6:8. Be mindful of acting just, enabling kindness, and always being humble of heart.

~~~~~~~~~~~~

Lord Jesus, help me to follow Your directives, which You mapped out so clearly in the Scriptures. I pray to rend my heart and mind to You, O Lord, that You may edify my life by Your Gospel. "Then He opened their minds to understand the Scriptures" (see Luke 24:45). Amen.

Be sober-minded; be watchful. Your adversary the devil prowls around like a roaring lion, seeking someone to devour. Resist him, firm in your faith, knowing that the same kinds of suffering are being experienced by your brotherhood throughout the world.

—1 Peter 5:8–9 ESV

- - - - - - - - - - -

*D*eer have their senses attuned to their environment at all times. These sensors don't work as a separate unit, but an integrated system designed to operate from within feet up to hundreds of yards away. If a deer is distracted, this will throw a curve in their alertness, allowing a hunter to possibly enjoy venison stew. We must also be on alert with a watchful, prayerful stance, for our adversary also keeps his glance upon our faltering faith.

Fear not, since we have been given the power to stand firm against the wiles of the devil. The more we walk in faith, while trusting in the promises of God, the more we will perceive that suffering experienced in this life will not be the final word. The enemy bargains on believers falling prey to their fears, hardships, and persecution, which will influence the deception of one's soul back to a sin state. However, there is strength in numbers, and together in Christ, we can celebrate our victory by the authority and power we share in the "empty tomb."

Do you believe there is a real spiritual enemy seeking to kill, steal, and destroy you? Resisting Satan and his schemes involves standing firm with the sword of the Spirit, which is your Bible. Be clear-minded to be spiritually vigilant, so you are prepared for any unwarranted attacks. Take heed that our placement in heaven is secured with your Father. The adversary wants to shake your godly submission while undermining God's goodness in your heart.

Thwart him by focusing on standing in faith, surrendering with obedience, and being confident in the blessed assurance of God's promises. If God is for you, who can be against you? (Romans 8:31).

Action Step of Faith: Begin to understand any triggers that make you falter or question your Christian walk. Be aware that God loves you and desires for you to enjoy your life abundantly. Be on the alert for the speaking serpent roaming in the garden of your mind.

~ ~ ~ ~ ~ ~ ~ ~ ~ ~ ~ ~

God of Grace, help me to remain aware of my actions, behaviors, and language so I don't return to any old, backslidden ways. I pray to set my gaze upon Jesus, who is always by my side; the Holy Spirit, who is my internal guide; and my Father in heaven, my eternal prize. Amen.

DAY 70

So, as God's own chosen people, who are holy [set apart, sanctified for His purpose] and well-beloved [by God Himself], put on a heart of compassion, kindness, humility, gentleness, and patience [which has the power to endure whatever injustice or unpleasantness comes, with good temper]; bearing graciously with one another, and willingly forgiving each other if one has a cause for complaint against another; just as the Lord has forgiven you, so should you forgive.
—Colossians 3:12–13 AMP

～～～～～～～～～～

*T*he term *forgive* is an action word that requires some movement on our part. A working definition is "to instruct oneself to stop feeling angry or resentful toward someone for an offense, flaw, or mistake." True forgiveness must be an effectuated act in order to exonerate another and allow them to experience God's consecrated purpose. The more unresolved baggage you carry throughout life, the more you create a heaviness of your burdened soul enslaved with bitterness, resentment, and unrelenting unwillingness to grant clemency. An unchecked ability to offer a pardon to another is a gateway to a hardened condition of the heart.

The apostle Paul is instructing the church at Colossae to impart Christian virtues to the believing community, including the art of forgiveness. He admonished the church that, as the Lord's chosen people, when they are wronged and betrayed, the expectation is for them to exemplify Jesus' model. Christians are called to forgive others as they have received absolution for their unfaithfulness to Christ. Forgiveness for some can be an acquired taste, as it can leave some with bitterness, while for others it can be the sweet flavor of victory on your palate.

Are you able to forgive those who hurt you with freedom, or have you become bound to a pit of revenge? Being sanctified in Christ adorns your heart to be reclothed with compassion, kindness, patience, and humility. You are able to endure the pain at another's hand by knitting your heart, allowing it to be stitched back together, while being weaved by God's love. Forgiveness doesn't vindicate the offense, but it dethrones the injustice from taking first place in your spirit. *"Be kind to one another, tenderhearted, forgiving one another, as God in Christ forgave you"* (Ephesians 4:32 ESV).

Action Step of Faith: Forgive today so that tomorrow you can be found free! Confess any unresolved unforgiveness you still bear, then receive God's full pardon as you forgive those who have maltreated you completely. Then place them in the mighty hands of your Father as you walk away sanctified!

~ ~ ~ ~ ~ ~ ~ ~ ~ ~ ~ ~

Merciful Jesus, help me to forgive those who have injured my soul, whether by physical, emotional, mental, or sexual abuse. Prayerfully, Father God, I ask You to supernaturally teach me how to love them with a full heart of compassion. Amen.

_____

_____

_____

_____

_____

_____

_____

_____

_____

_____

_____

_____

Jesus responded, "Beloved daughter, your faith in me has released your healing. You may go with my peace."

—Luke 8:48 TPT

~ ~ ~ ~ ~ ~ ~ ~ ~ ~ ~

*O*ur internal dialogue is just as vital to our human psyche as what we audibly speak over our lives. Typically, what you believe to be your truth will restore you or splinter within you. Our daily self-conversations lay the framework for a sound mind that's able to partner with the Holy Architect to attain a healthy body. Even when we vacate these earthly tents, those who believe will receive a glorified body that no longer can be touched by disease.

The synoptic gospels provide an account of a women who suffered from a twelve-year disorder that caused an issue of blood. Even after she sought healing for countless years from the physicians of that time, no one could cure her hemorrhaging disease. She had heard of the miracles of Jesus, and she "knew" that what was within this Healer would unlock the antidote for complete restoration. As soon as she pressed through the crowd, she reached out for the hem of His garment, and Jesus felt the healing power escape from His body. This woman came trembling before the presence of the Lord, declaring it was she who had touched Him. Jesus then relayed to her, and to the jeering crowd, that it was her faith that made her well, which not only brought outer healing, but inner peace. Jesus made it personal as He responded to her as a beloved daughter.

Do you know the Great Physician? When you can speak life into your mind, body, and spirit through the foundational belief of faith, miracles take place. You first need to trust God for who He is and understand that His desire is for you to have a blessed life no matter the diagnosis. Your worldly battle occurs in your thoughts and actions, which can be a roadblock to your greatest breakthroughs. Knowing God intimately sets a precedent for a deep relationship with communication immersed in prayer. Prayer doesn't always change our situations, health reports, or difficult issues, but it effects change within our internal contemplation.

Action Step of Faith: Trust God with something you are struggling with today. Place either yourself or someone you care about into the healing hands of the Father. Lay claim to the fact that He will co-labor in this season with you, whether in the miracle of a clean bill of health or in the promise of eternity.

~~~~~~~~~~~~

Jehovah Rapha, help me to trust You completely with my health condition or that of a loved one today. Prayerfully, I tarry for the report of the Lord, saturated with a fervent, unwavering faith only secured in You. Amen.

_____
_____
_____
_____
_____
_____
_____
_____
_____
_____
_____
_____
_____
_____
_____
_____
_____
_____

Then he brought them out and asked, "Sirs, what must I do to be saved?" They replied, "Believe in the Lord Jesus and you will be saved, along with everyone in your household."
—Acts 16:30–31 NLT

*A*s humans, we can be found guilty by association or innocent by disassociation, depending on our intended designation. The crowd with whom we choose to associate is a marker with respect to our character, affiliation, and persuasion. There is an old adage that states that the one driving the getaway car is as culpable as the one robbing the bank. In our culture, we are judged and grouped according to our social circles.

Paul and Silas knew firsthand about the outcomes of being missionaries, spreading the Good News of the Gospel. Not everyone was welcoming of their proclamations, and eventually they got to experience a very unwelcoming response landing them in jail, physically beaten, stripped, and imprisoned. However, that environment became their sphere of influence for Jesus to show up in a mighty way. They began singing praises to the Lord, as their joy was unapologetic and unabashed. This resulted in the earth quaking, which unlocked the prison doors, shook the foundations, and loosened their shackles. The jailer was so frightened that he wanted to know their mighty Lord intimately, and he was saved, as well as his entire household. An unlikely setback for a holy setup, whereby he was set free!

Do you know that you embody the power and authority to represent yourself as the victorious overcomer in Christ? You can be a world changer, starting in your own living room, for those around you daily. Residing within you is the Holy Ghost power ready to verify your words, actions, and language of how Christ has transformed your life. Prayerfully, you are never placed in chains for your faith, but through your belief, you are no longer a slave to sin, but a child of God.

Action Step of Faith: How often do you step out of your comfort zone to share the Good News of the Gospel? Practice sharing your testimony in under ten minutes to be able to place a much-needed transformational foot in someone's door!

~ ~ ~ ~ ~ ~ ~ ~ ~ ~ ~ ~

Lord Jesus, I pray to be a witness in this world for those who don't recognize Your goodness and aren't yet adopted into the Kingdom. Today, place Your words on my lips so I might be that powerful witness to the lost, broken, and afflicted on Your behalf. Amen.

_____
_____
_____
_____
_____
_____
_____
_____
_____
_____
_____
_____
_____
_____
_____
_____

DAY
73

> Trust in the LORD with all your heart and
> lean not on your own understanding; in all
> your ways submit to him, and he will make
> your paths straight.
>
> —Proverbs 3:5–6 NIV

*H*ow often have you heard the phrase, "We make plans, and God laughs"? For years, I was under the misapprehension that I had the wheel of control over my circumstances while steering the trail of my outcomes. To be transparent, I still attempt to be the pilot of my destination as I assign Jesus the passenger seat. What still waters lie deep within us as humans that we feel entitled to take dominion over God's intended fate. Christians need to cooperate rather than moderate their God-ordained memoirs.

Submissiveness to God is glorious, and trusting Him fully is divine. When we can subordinate our own understanding to the Lord, that is where reverence and fear converge. This requires not so much a cerebral knowing but a heart nature of deep reliance to the Holy One. The full depth of knowledge that is solely dependent, along with a full reliance, on Him will lead to the right, steadfast course to attainment. One's morality will steer the eyes to be fixed on the straight and narrow road ahead.

Who is the administrator of your choices, decisions, and perceptions? In shifting your plans forward, do you consult with the holy team of the Father, Son, and Holy Spirit? Or rather do you take it under your own advisement? To be wise is to consult with your Master Creator on all things that concern your life. The rubber meets the road of your servant journey where it intersects at the foot of the cross as you daily submit yourself to the Lord.

Action Step of Faith: Take a quick scan over your greatest successes and your most painful fails. Where has God moved but you have intervened on His behalf? God uses all things for good either way, but by submitting to Him, you will begin to decipher the difference with definitive lessons learned.

~~~~~~~~~~~~

Almighty God, teach me to posture as a submissive being so I can place my life fully in Your hands. Prayerfully, Lord, may my life be an expression of my love for You. Amen.

_____

_____

_____

_____

_____

_____

_____

_____

_____

_____

_____

_____

_____

_____

_____

_____

_____

_____

_____

_____

DAY
74

*O Lord my God, I cried to You for help, and
You healed me.*

—Psalm 30:2 NASB

~~~~~~~~~~~

*T*here have been times in my life when I would have to reach
out to a doctor or specialist for healing, especially when my
younger son was very ill. He struggled through a season of severe
asthma and issues with breathing. Talk about stopping the heart of
a parent while grasping for a lifeline of answers. Over the years, my
first line of defense has been turning to the Lord. He is the Holy
One of healing whom I immediately dial up through my cries of
prayer, whether for my family, the Body of Christ, or myself.

The psalmist was familiar with the undeniable posture of
seeking the restorative care of his Lord. David sang songs of praise
with personal thanksgiving for God's curative touch. The extolling
of the goodness and greatness of health and strength was reserved
by this singer only for his Savior. David's physical situation was
precarious, but God alone kept him breathing so he did not perish
in the pit.

It is good to have gratitude for your earthly doctors and
medications, but do you lift your hands of praise daily to the
Great Physician? Every dawn the Lord awakens you is a good day
to count your blessings! You were born into this world with an
unknown expiration date assigned by the Lord. Live fully, as none
of us know the hour of our last breath, and love deeply, as tomorrow is not promised. Keep praying with believing, while trusting
and receiving your healing at the altar of grace.

Action Step of Faith: Be accountable to God to take care of yourself as He wonderfully and fearfully created you. When you are ill, physically or mentally, first cry out to your Healer and receive the holy prescription for your well-being.

~~~~~~~~~~~~

Lord of Mercy, touch me with Your healing hand to cure my disease, whether it is in my heart, in my physical body, or in an attitude of despair. Let the meditation of my heart always give You praise, honor, and glory, for You are my Deliverer. Amen.

DAY
75

- - - - - - - - - - -

*H*ow often have you heard this worldly expression, "I got a guy for that"! It's not the greatest use of the English language, but I believe you get the drift. For some reason, our earthly stature dotes on the measurement of those we have in our prospective posse. However, the quantity usually outweighs the quality of those who are unfailing in palpable times of need. Only our God is forever faithful to stand beside us, while others rebuke us in condemnation as we profess our holy vindication.

Our Lord is our Savior because we have been redeemed by His blood at Calvary through the final victory at the cross. Jesus protects His people while defeating every enemy strike, no matter how powerful, continual, or intolerable. As He opposes our adversaries, the children of God can rest in their inherited peace, their stance of righteousness, and their security, all established through Christ alone. This is the steadfast compassion of the Lord, with the sealed promise to those who call upon His mighty name.

Do you live in a state of contempt by the lashing tongue or the fist of another? The Lord's Word tells you that no weapon formed against you, whether verbally or physically, can thrive, as Jesus is your vindicator. Your chains are loosed as you declare the blood of Christ to bind the adversary, and he will flee. Today is the day of recompense for those who come against you, as the Lord's heritage is Your eternal ally.

Action Step of Faith: Spend more time surrounding yourself with those who truly love you rather than those you are hoping someday will. Know that God cares for your well-being as He places a "hedge of protection" around you. Be vigilant to judiciously remain under His advisement.

~~~~~~~~~~~~

Gracious Lord, help me to stay under Your wing of protection and not falter by the decisions made by my freewill thinking. Jehovah Nissi, my Defender, forever keep Your shield of protection over my life while guarding my heart and mind in Christ Jesus. Amen.

_____
_____
_____
_____
_____
_____
_____
_____
_____
_____
_____
_____
_____
_____
_____
_____
_____
_____
_____
_____

DAY 76

I lift up my eyes to the hills. From where does my help come? My help comes from the LORD, who made heaven and earth.
—Psalm 121:1–2 ESV

~~~~~~~~~~~~

*T*he stately mountain views throughout this country are beautiful and quite majestic. The closer we approach the distinctive peaks, the more they seem to overwhelm our personal physique. Can you ponder that the glorious Creator who formed them into shape is the same Holy One from where our help comes?

The psalmist reminds us in this verse that we should set our gaze upon the Lord for our help in difficult situations. Jesus embodies compassion for our fears and worries, as He is in full control. As believers, we can rest assured, knowing that God is forever mighty while sitting on His sovereign throne. Each day we get a new supply of sufficient grace coupled with mercies afresh at the break of morning.

How often do you invite Jesus to assist when your pilgrimage of faith is troubled? You were not fashioned to take this excursion alone, but you were meant to incorporate the aid of the Lord. When Christ resides within you, there is an Indweller helping you to navigate through the perilous times you will encounter. Look to the heavens instead of your circumstances, seek counsel from on high rather than below, and trust that your help only generates from the King of Kings and the Lord of Lords.

Action Step of Faith: Lean into God as He inclines unto you. Be mindful of where your help comes from when you are tormented, tattered, and torn. Trust the Lord as He deeply cares for you.

~~~~~~~~~~~~

Merciful God, thank You that You are my ever-present help in intervals of distress. Lord, meet me in the season of my crisis before I weaken to outreach any other source. *Great is Thy faithfulness, Lord, unto me.* Amen.

DAY 77

*"Father, if You are willing, take this cup from
Me. Yet not My will, but Yours be done."*
—Luke 22:42 BSB

~~~~~~~~~~~

*T*hrowing darts is a game of skill whereby the aim is to hit a
bull's-eye target in the center of the board. Being able to hit
the optimal central area requires much focus, practice, and willing
determination. Submissiveness to the Lord is an inclination with
our complete focus on Jesus being at the center of everything we
do, as His will is our aim. When we keep Him as our fulcrum
point, we can balance our lives according to His intended decrees
as we continually try to hit the holy mark.

In the book of Luke, Jesus consciously, voluntarily, and
obediently *"endured the cross, despising the shame"* (Hebrews 12:2
ESV). Even though He was in agony, His will bent in accordance
with that of His Father's on our behalf. He knew that His mission
would be our redemption, as Jesus could be the only acceptable
sacrifice to cover the sins of this world, both then and now. Luke
described that the sweat from His brow became drops of blood,
which emphasized the intensity of the trauma to the Son of Man.
Nevertheless, He climbed that tree, for it was the will of God to
give His only begotten Son, so that those who believe in Him
would not perish but have eternal life (John 3:16).

Do you know Your heavenly Father's will for your life? It is
vital to nurture your relationship with Jesus Christ daily so as to
reveal God's will and way forward. You will never endure the agony
and ecstasy of a holy design, but inclining to His passionate plan is
key to discovering your God-breathed essence. Remaining on the
narrow pavement will be your survival path to God's envisioned
objective.

Action Step of Faith: Exercise your restraint from worldly endeavors to attain godly treasures manifested from an obedient lifestyle. The more you converse with your Creator, the more apt you are to unwrap your gift of Kingdom purpose.

~~~~~~~~~~~~~

Dear Lord, I pray to seek You so Your will be done and not my own. Holy Spirit, guide me along my holy voyage through this life as I gaze upon the focal point, which is Christ, each and every day. Amen.

_____

_____

_____

_____

_____

_____

_____

_____

_____

_____

_____

_____

_____

_____

_____

_____

_____

_____

_____

_____

_____

_____

DAY 78

For I am convinced that neither death nor life, neither angels nor demons, neither the present nor the future, nor any powers, neither height nor depth, nor anything else in all creation, will be able to separate us from the love of God that is in Christ Jesus our Lord.

—Romans 8:38–39 NIV

~~~~~~~~~~~

*F*or those who have enjoyed a long-term matrimonial state of bliss, I celebrate you! When taking your vows before family and friends, you are also entering into a covenant of three with the Lord. The expectant hope for a new marriage is for endurance regardless of sickness, poverty, or turbulent times. A marriage made in Christ is truly engrafted as the image of a three-stranded cord. However, human love is never to be compared with the perfect love of God.

The apostle Paul speaks in confidence that nothing will separate our love that our Father bestows upon us. No matter the demonic plagues or iron-fisted rulers in any space of time, nothing will sever our relationship with almighty God. The Lord's love for His children is immeasurable by any depth, width, or height determination. There is no authority under heaven that can cut the binding *agape* tie of the Bridegroom to His Bride. Not even the redeemed can separate themselves from His loving care as He has secured our salvation forever. Salvation alone is the work only of God in and through us.

Do you know the unshakable, unbreakable, and unmatchable love of the Father? Even if you turned away from Him, Jesus continues to remain faithful to His promises as God cannot deny Himself. Perhaps others in your life have promised a "forever" love and reneged. Be ever so cognizant not to attach the attributes of Jesus to a mortal passion. His love is everlasting and steadfast; however, human hearts are deceptive, leaving behind the wreckage of tattered, broken pledges. God's love never fails.

Action Step of Faith: Meditate on the love of Christ as you deeply receive in a profound new way. Walk in the truth of His adoration so you can pour out to others from your overflowing wellspring of compassion.

～～～～～～～～～～～～

Loving God, I pray to always gravitate under Your wing of salvation and Your heartbeat of love that You impart daily. Lord, may I return that love with my own offering of gratitude, adoration, confession, and praise by each momentary breath. Amen.

DAY 79

"I am the vine, you are the branches; he who
abides in Me and I in him, he bears much fruit,
for apart from Me you can do nothing."
—John 15:5 NASB

- - - - - - - - - - -

*I*n our culture, we expeditiously chase after many aspirations,
goals, and dreams. Many times, we pursue them in wild abandon to grasp what we crave, which might not always be profitable. Society tends to place value upon titles, whether it be one of
betrothal, boss, or bounteous degrees. The title to which I humbly
cleave is "child of God," which avails itself to achieve any foundational ascent.

This verse is such a beautiful illustration that depicts our
symbiotic relationship with Christ. The word *abide* means "to
steadfastly reside in a place." When we abide in the Lord, He
abides in us. This is the continual personal relationship with Jesus
portrayed by trust, obedience, prayer, and joy. Apart from God,
we cannot bear any valuable fruit for the Kingdom, as the world
produces nothing of eternal worth.

What is your identification, first and foremost, of who you
are? So often, and without hesitation, it is a worldly recognition.
First, acknowledge the Holy Spirit who dwells within you, then
bend unto Him, and your account will be a powerful witness
to His glory. To align your life with Christ will transform your
desires, ambitions, and mindset to be in collaboration with the
Holy One who inhabits your heart. Inadvertently, what you hold
in high esteem will hold you.

Action Step of Faith: Decree and declare your adoption into the household of heaven. Let your first title be your last, and that will secure everything in between to be entitled by God.

~~~~~~~~~~~~

Holy Spirit, I pray to notice Your leading in my life and the master plan scribed on my behalf. Lord Jesus, I lift my holy hands in praise of thanksgiving, honor, and joy for the friend I have in You. Amen.

_____
_____
_____
_____
_____
_____
_____
_____
_____
_____
_____
_____
_____
_____
_____
_____
_____
_____
_____
_____
_____
_____

*But we belong to God, and those who know God
listen to us. If they do not belong to God, they do
not listen to us. That is how we know if someone
has the Spirit of truth or the spirit of deception.*
—1 John 4:6 NLT

*I*f you have children, perhaps you will relate to this plight. How
often do we provide gems of wisdom to our kids, only to be
informed that as parents we are clueless? Meanwhile, the same
information that was deemed worthless is now received by another's tongue, which has been celebrated as genius. Sometimes you
just want to give up, because our households tend not to receive
our parental intel while embracing an outsider's statement as fact.

If you take this example of shared knowledge to those you
love, while exhorting the Gospel, it might fall on the deaf ears
of the unchurched. People who don't believe are deceived as they
resist sound doctrine. The Word of the Lord doesn't make sense
to them or conform to the pattern of their worldly existence. The
Spirit of Truth whom the blood-bought believers embrace, the
Spirit of deception wants to erase. Even Jesus was not accepted in
His own neighborhood, so you are not alone.

Do you take "no" as a final answer from those who you evan-
gelize? The more you receive and experience the goodness of God,
the more you ache to share His gift of salvation. However, even
Jesus had to wipe the dust off His sandals (Matthew 10:14). Offer
them to God through the light of love that emulates your witness.
Shine brightly in the darkened caverns of your own living room
and kitchen table. Unceasingly pray for those who have shut their
hearts and ears to the Holy One of Truth. You are a seed planter for
the Lord, but only Jesus can save and water their souls.

Action Step of Faith: Love those who don't always regard your enthusiasm for Jesus. Guard yourself in prayer from those who might scoff at your faith, so you can continue to stand affirmed with a glowing verity.

~~~~~~~~~~~~~

Father God, prayerfully help me to never hoard the gift of Your redemption but to share it with all whom I encounter. Spirit, speak through me as an obedient vessel of honor on assignment for You. Amen.

_____

_____

_____

_____

_____

_____

_____

_____

_____

_____

_____

_____

_____

_____

_____

_____

_____

_____

_____

_____

_____

_____

_____

_____

_____

DAY 81

And that water is a picture of baptism, which now saves you, not by removing dirt from your body, but as a response to God from a clean conscience. It is effective because of the resurrection of Jesus Christ.

—1 Peter 3:21 NLT

~~~~~~~~~~~

*T*here is nothing like a refreshing shower after a long, hot day outside working in the garden. Experiencing your sweat intermingling with the dirt from digging outdoors feels as though you are unclean from crown to toe. The washing with soap and water cleanses our earthly covering. The only true way to be cleansed from the inside out is by the regeneration of the baptismal waters. Baptism is an essential symbol of God's grace upon us.

In Peter's first letter, he is drawing upon that, not just by the passing of waters over us, but by the internal confession of forgiveness that we can be saved with a responsive "good conscience." *Baptism*, which in the Greek means "to drown," signifies our immersion into new life in Christ alone. The saving grace symbolized here is only affected by the resurrection power evidenced by an empty grave. A working definition for *baptism* is "an outward expression of an inward reality of holy change." For the body of believers, we share in His victory over sin, as we are victorious overcomers depicted by the finished work at the cross.

Have you experienced baptism for the forgiveness of sins? Have you been brought up through the waters of regeneration in your new life with Christ? What a powerful declaration to make a public profession of your faith to God, for God, and with God before the elect of Christ. This act of transformation is a work of the Spirit, as it is only received by the grace of the Lord.

Action Step of Faith: Have you professed your faith through the action of baptism? Speak with your pastor or shepherd if you feel led by the Lord to declare a readied testimony that gives God all the glory as you prepare for immersion.

~ ~ ~ ~ ~ ~ ~ ~ ~ ~ ~ ~

Holy Spirit, let me remember my baptism and recall my gratitude to partake by Your example. Lord, lead me to the waters of purification, if that is Your will and way for my life, as I pray for those to be washed by the waters of Your saving grace. Amen.

_____

_____

_____

_____

_____

_____

_____

_____

_____

_____

_____

_____

_____

_____

_____

_____

_____

_____

_____

_____

"Watch and pray that you may not enter into temptation. The spirit indeed is willing, but the flesh is weak."

—Matthew 26:41 ESV

I myself am a longtime weight watcher and a healthy nutrition enthusiast. However, when chocolate mousse and fried chicken are in the atmosphere, all bets are off. The delicious aroma, decadent taste, and alluring presentation is a feast alone to our subdued human senses, which unwittingly suffer a gluttonous outcome. There is a remedy for this, called self-discipline, and we are bestowed it through our spiritual fruits.

Even Jesus experienced forty days of wilderness temptation in His encounter with the evil one. He had prayed and fasted vigorously with humility, and thus should be our attainment of restraint. Jesus would always lay His life down before His Father in complete and utter surrender. The tempter tested Christ with worldly values to only be cast out by His sword of the Spirit. Today's verse underscores Jesus' time of preparation to accomplish the culmination of His life's mission, which bankrupted heaven on our behalf. The offer of temptation can deny our new birthrights if not prayerfully declined, denied, and disavowed.

What is the subtle whispering in your ear that leads you astray? The father of deception will use whatever means he can to target your weakest areas of mortal enticement. Discern your flesh-filled land mines of desire to shift your will toward godly virtues of fortitude. Know the pitfalls that tempt your fate so you can pray with intentionality and authority in Christ.

Action Step of Faith: As you continue on your faith journey, know that you will be tempted to veer off your holy path countered by appealing invitations, pretty smiles, and financially beneficial destinations. Each has its own cost of collateral damage to your soul. Be vigilant to always "watch and pray."

~~~~~~~~~~~~~

Father God, alert my spirit to convict my thoughts to remain in alignment with Your master plan for my life. Lord, may my ascent pursue glory, forever fixed on holy habits, rather than a descent into worldly cravings. Amen.

DAY 83

*Not only that, but we rejoice in our sufferings,
knowing that suffering produces endurance, and
endurance produces character, and character produces hope, and hope does not put us to shame,
because God's love has been poured into our hearts
through the Holy Spirit who has been given to us.*
—Romans 5:3–5 ESV

~~~~~~~~~~~

*S*teadfast endurance requires a consistent action of unwavering movement pressing forward. Several years ago, I was actively pursuing getting my bodily temple into tiptop shape while working with a physical trainer. To be successful in reaching a goal in this realm necessitated an intensity for persistent motivation. Of course, there were those days when I just wanted to retreat to the couch, but I leaned in to reach the mark toward my goal. Employing a trainer provided personal coaching while supporting my best interests at heart. Meanwhile, this was the navigational pull to the finish line regardless of the difficulty, pain, and levels of challenge.

The apostle Paul was the Roman encourager in that period, affirming the Church firmly that those justified in their faith had an unshakeable hope. God's people could rest assured, while rejoicing in the persecutions, trials, and sufferings, that tribulation formed strong character. This transformation process was their sandpaper to buff the hard edges of the heart and reconfigure the mind to bear witness to Christ. For on the day of judgment, believers will not fear humiliation, for we belong to God, as the Holy Spirit has been poured out upon our converted souls.

How is your faith journey advancing presently? Notice the growth spurts of perseverance when you are faced with troubling times. Your character will modify its Spirit-filled attitude by its altered conversion of holy latitude. Grasp joy fully, regardless of any fear or trepidation! Give God all the glory for the Spirit that resides within, which is the eternal assurance of an engrafted hope to endure.

Action Step of Faith: Take account of how circumstances once defined you, in comparison to how you define your circumstances matured in Christ. Continue to press through your mess, as it will shape you into a warrior for Christ.

~~~~~~~~~~~~

Father God, help me to remain firm on the road of salvation while You sculpt my heart and readjust my mind during intervals of affliction. Lord, thank You that You are always with me, not only on the mountaintops but also in the valley seasons. Amen.

_____
_____
_____
_____
_____
_____
_____
_____
_____
_____
_____
_____
_____
_____
_____
_____
_____
_____
_____

Now repent of your sins and turn to God, so that your sins may be wiped away. Then times of refreshment will come from the presence of the Lord, and He will again send you Jesus, your appointed Messiah.

—Acts 3:19–20 NLT

T he shampoo industry has placed upon each bottle clear instructions on how to apply their products. Simply put, it is to "wash, rinse, repeat." Once we complete that arduous process, our hair should feel clean, renewed, and pleasant to the touch. However, if you don't have many locks, massaging one's scalp can stimulate the hair follicles to prosper once again. This formula is an analogy to beseech forgiveness as we repent, return, refresh, and revive ourselves back to God. In our contrite heart, we seek Jesus to cleanse us by His blood while rinsing our souls with holy pardon, as we will repeat this over and over again throughout our redemptive story.

In the book of Acts, Peter is preaching his second sermon, calling the Jews to repentance of their rejection of Jesus as Messiah. He explicitly tells them to ask for forgiveness and turn back to God instead of continuing to run in the opposing direction. Peter promised three important results of this act, which included: forgiveness of sins, a time of refreshing in their indwelling spirits, and the promise of the second coming of the Christ. This is the invitation that is still available to those who don't believe. This refreshing is life-altering for those who are adopted into the Kingdom of Heaven.

Have you received your time of refreshment found at the feet of Jesus? Bask in the presence of the Lord with genuine repentance and obedient faith, which will produce unspeakable peace. Jesus took your guilt and shame and bore it upon Himself on the cross. It is not yours to carry anymore. Repent, return, refresh, revive!

Action Step of Faith: Remand to God what you were never meant to bear so you can have your "guilt-ridden" weights removed from your unrelenting conscience. Let this day be renewed as you bear your burdens unto the Lord and entrust them into His mighty hands. Request forgiveness, receive forgiveness, and rest in being forgiven, child of God.

~~~~~~~~~~~~

Gracious Lord, I come to You with a contrite heart and bow before You in a posture of forgiveness of sins. I pray to fully receive Your pardon, as I extend my discipline of fully loving those who have not fully forgiven me. Help me to love the unlovely and forgive freely as Jesus has so graciously done on my behalf. Amen.

*And let us not grow weary while doing good,
for in due season we shall reap if we do not lose
heart. Therefore, as we have opportunity, let us
do good to all, especially to those who are of the
household of faith.*

—Galatians 6:9–10 NKJV

~~~~~~~~~~~

*F*or those who have given birth, whether in the physical sense or in a literal platitude, staying the course is vital. Bringing something forth to existence requires complete steadfastness even in the midst of weariness. As a mother-to-be is instructed to bear down to deliver, it is the preeminence of reaping of new life weaved by our Master Creator. For a business owner to commence a new venture, many hours of blood, sweat, and tears are emitted through the grueling process to glean a ripe harvest. As in the infamous tale of the race between the tortoise and the hare, slow and steady is a winning strategy.

Paul urges the church in Galatia to continue doing good work as that is consistent with their beliefs. Remaining focused on others, while cooperating with the power of the Holy Spirit's guidance, will bear profitable fruit. Our faith must also be constituted by an outpouring of servitude and hospitality for the long haul. Our eternal life comes from planting seeds of the Spirit and not from fleshy proclivities. As we await our heavenly rewards, we are called to impart good to all we encounter, whether in or out of our comfortable Sunday pews.

How do you serve God in or out of your household of faith? Jesus was our example of serving others, as He came to serve, not be served, as He gave His life as a ransom for many (Matthew 20:28). Your Bible is a blueprint for living a Christian lifestyle. Even in your exhaustion, persist with your holy witness, as your word offers refreshing for your heart to beat forward. Faithfully, standing firm first requires a perpetual stance of "leaning in."

Action Step of Faith: Always serve others with the joy of the Lord so you leave a pleasing aroma trailing behind. Do no harm to anyone, but respectfully lead with kindness and open arms. Check your heart at the door before occupying another's airspace.

~~~~~~~~~~~~

Lord Jesus, teach me to serve like Martha with the heart of Mary. May my compassion rise up to meet Your holy expectation as I model Your perfect example of love. Prayerfully, infill within my spirit the unending passion to serve Your people effortlessly. Amen.

_____
_____
_____
_____
_____
_____
_____
_____
_____
_____
_____
_____
_____
_____
_____
_____
_____
_____
_____
_____
_____

DAY
86

Let the words of my mouth and the medita-
tion of my heart be acceptable in your sight, O
LORD, *my rock and my redeemer.*
—Psalm 19:14 ESV

----

*M*editation is a practice in which an individual uses a
technique such as mindfulness or focusing on one
distinct object. There exist several avenues of exploration in this
genre, but let's travel on the specific road of prayer and worship.
Worship is an entryway that ushers in the presence of the Holy
Spirit manifested in our atmosphere. This is the focal point of
access to meditate fully on Jesus Christ being ever so near to you.
Prayerfully, the more we encounter the living God, the more we
can be mindful of our language and hearts and be found pleasing
in His sight.

God supplies His gift of grace to us, which is defined as
unmerited favor. There is no store or online mecca that could offer
it, but Christ's supply is sufficient enough. One way I can describe
grace is a perfectly illustrated dance with Jesus, step in step, completely in rhythm, while in sync, as He adores us harmoniously.
The words that we speak on His behalf, as the psalmist bequests,
should always reflect a suitable act of worship before God as we
receive His grace.

Are your words and heart connected in honoring God? Truly
it's the theme of the dance to seamlessly prevail. When trouble
comes to interrupt you, how do you react? Focus back into your
prayer place so your holy space doesn't become contaminated with
toxic issues. Each day, may your tongue remain in step with your
witness as your heart uniformly complements your actions. Keep
standing upon the Rock, as He is your redeeming King.

Action Step of Faith: Your words and actions define you as the world watches you falter in your faith. Your recovery is found through repentance as we are freely forgiven by the Father, who loves you. Get back up, dust yourself off, and return to the dance with Jesus, who is waiting for you!

~~~~~~~~~~~~~

My Jesus, I thank You that You loved me first, and so much so that you freely gave Your life for mine! May our rhythm dance never be out of sync, and may my lips always profess my adoration for my King. Amen.

_____
_____
_____
_____
_____
_____
_____
_____
_____
_____
_____
_____
_____
_____
_____
_____
_____
_____
_____
_____
_____

DAY 87

For the grace of God has appeared, bringing salvation to all men, instructing us to deny ungodliness and worldly desires and to live sensibly, righteously and godly in the present age, looking for the blessed hope and the appearing of the glory of our great God and Savior, Christ Jesus, who gave Himself for us to redeem us from every lawless deed, and to purify for Himself a people for His own possession, zealous for good deeds.
—Titus 2:11–14 NASB

~~~~~~~~~~~~

*M*any years ago, there was a program known for highlighting the lifestyles of those who acquired fame, fortune, and extravagant material gain. The host would flagrantly flaunt their posh palaces and cosmopolitan cultures as if that was the ultimate way to define a life well lived. A true interpretation of who someone "is" should not be predicated on what they "have." The wealth of those who place their treasures in heavenly equity will yield a Kingdom return for a lifestyle of faith.

This verse of scripture is the Gospel's balance sheet delineating a holy doctrine of eternal disciplines. Christians are trained and approved by the saving work of God's grace to instruct those who have not yet received this transformation power. The grace that has brought us out of the miry pit can be the hope of salvation for those praying to vacate a darkened existence. Only though Christ do we realize the urgency to renounce sin, lawlessness, and ungodliness, to pursue a lifestyle of holiness while tarrying for the second coming of our Lord.

How are you living for Christ as you abide eagerly for His return? Each day you arise is another opportunity to define yourself by the evidence of your holy character. This is a rich lifestyle that the Lord bestows upon you from the storehouses of heaven. Forever famous be found in His eyes, which loved you first, as He handcrafted His child! Your daily conflict is an internal warring between your prior flesh and your transformed mind. Be zealous to do good works for Christ so you may stake your claim with the God who loves you.

Action Step of Faith: What you put into your daily relationship with Jesus will be the example of a life well lived, substantiating your conversion. Meditate upon these words as a point of reference for upright conduct as you wait upon the Lord. Stay alert if you recognize a return to old habits to avoid a slippery slope descent. Anchor your heart to your blessed hope of assurance.

~~~~~~~~~~~~

Father God, my hope is only found in Your loving hands. Prayerfully, may my passion for right living never be tempted by worldly desires or my feet be found on the shifting sands of this culture. May I always keep seeking the way, the truth, and the life for steadfast endurance daily. Amen.

_____
_____
_____
_____
_____
_____
_____
_____
_____
_____
_____
_____
_____
_____
_____
_____

Now faith is the assurance of things hoped for,
the conviction of things not seen.
—Hebrews 11:1 ESV

The time of the year that I anxiously await is the captivating season of autumn. God's paintbrush wielding gorgeous hues of gold, brown, orange, and red makes nature's perfect canvas glorious. The soft fall winds begin to blow in the breeze as you can smell the apples bursting and the corn roasting in the air. When the wind moves though our hair as it blows the leaves out of newly raked piles, we can't see it, but we feel its presence against us.

Our confident hope is grasped though a tangible belief! Just as faith is not a matter of blind trust propagated on what we haven't yet seen, we know that Christ lives. Our blessed assurance is not established in genies and wizards, but in a concrete, eternally trustworthy Lord who has revealed Himself though the resurrection. The mighty rushing wind of the *Ruach*—in Hebrew translated as "Holy Spirit"—dwells within each believer, while the conviction of our faith is palpable. To exult the name of Jesus, conjugated with His promises of eternity, is a consistent thread throughout the Bible. Fully trusting without seeing is pure Kingdom reality regenerated in the eyes of one's Spirit-filled heart.

How deep is your conviction? Do you question what you can't see or rest assured in what you have experienced in your faith walk? Knowing God intimately is derived through a relentless pursuit after a deep relationship with Jesus. His perfect love will cast out all your doubts and fears. The longer you are walking with your Creator, the less you negotiate His existence but embrace His unfailing love.

Action Step of Faith: When you hear God speak to you, listen to the that still, small voice. Be aware of His internal whispering to your spirit as the assurance of His presence is understood and undeniably felt.

~ ~ ~ ~ ~ ~ ~ ~ ~ ~ ~

Father God, prayerfully may I never cross-examine Your existence in my life while my total dependence upon You rests upon Your all-consuming love. Lord, may I always experience your presence that surrounds me as I walk by faith and not by sight. Amen.

*I correct and discipline everyone I love. So be
diligent and turn from your indifference. "Look!
I stand at the door and knock. If you hear my
voice and open the door, I will come in, and we
will share a meal together as friends."*
—Revelation 3:19–20 NLT

*A*s a parental figure, one must also be a disciplinarian.
It might not always be the favored part of rearing children, but it is a necessary entity. Instructing a child with correction,
constructive language, and reproof is vital to raise a morally viable
member of society. When these seeds of reproach are planted early
in one's youth, during maturation, the harvest will not produce
spoiled fruit. Start children off on the way they should go, and
even when they are old, they will not turn from it (Proverbs 22:6).

And so, the story continues, even for us, the matured
Christians, as well as the ones newly joining the journey. Our
heavenly Father will continue to correct and discipline us through
His imparted teachings whether from childhood or in our adult
status. Our loving Abba will reprove those whom He loves as He
convicts us to repent before the intervention of judgment becomes
a mighty paternal lesson. The Spirit woos us through prevenient
grace, as Jesus awaits our response, while personally standing by
the door of our hearts to be welcomed in.

Have you welcomed Him in? Do you nourish your relationship daily with God's mighty instruction, scriptures, and prayer?
The more you sup with the Lord, the deeper the revelation of who
you are in Christ becomes illuminated in your daily affirmations.
Taking this journey to uncover the edges, boundaries, and pitfalls
that keep you stuck in behaviors can be traced to wayward strongholds from years ago. This ninety-day spiritual inventory was

ignited to bestow "light bulb" moments of holy clarity to demolish any walls of lies, fears, traumas, and pain that has kept you from achieving your God-ordained destiny. A "known life" in Christ produces a "transformed life" by the Holy Spirit, and a "redeemed life" at the hand of your Father God.

Action Step of Faith: Love God, love humanity, and love yourself. Keep pressing, keep praying, and keep your eyes forever fixed on Jesus!

~~~~~~~~~~~

Dear Lord, instruct me, correct me, hold me, and love me forevermore. Prayerfully, Jesus, guide me along the pathways of this life, direct my steps on the narrow roadway, and protect me along this pilgrimage that leads directly to You. Amen.

_____

_____

_____

_____

_____

_____

_____

_____

_____

_____

_____

_____

_____

_____

_____

_____

May mercy, peace, and love be multiplied to you.
—Jude 1:2 ESV

----

*C*ongratulations, you have reached the top of the staircase of this devotional journey! Remain firmly on the landing to keep your newly transformed mind, heart, and behavior steeped in God's grace. But don't get too comfortable—there will always be a new elevation of staircases to ascend as we daily persevere and grow in Christ! Let us always remain teachable spirits while seeking, praying, persisting, and pursuing Jesus Christ in order to exemplify His virtues. Be aware of becoming frustrated, complacent, or weary in your walk, but endure for your Kingdom purpose even if you need to revisit Day 1 of this book.

The apostle Paul in the book of Romans supplies us with a plan for human salvation and a road map that leads to heaven. If your road trip on life's present highway has you gazing in the rearview mirror, reset your GPS and follow the "Romans Road" back to Christ:

All have sinned and fallen short of the glory of God (Romans 3:23).

God shows His love for us in that while we were still sinners, Christ died for us (Romans 5:8).

For the wages of sin is death, but the free gift of God is eternal life in Christ Jesus our Lord (Romans 6:23).

If you confess with your mouth that Jesus is Lord and believe in your heart that God

raised Him from the dead, you will be saved (Romans 10:9).

Everyone who calls on the name of the Lord will be saved (Romans 10:13).

Action Step of Faith: Reaffirm your faith by asking God to carve these Scriptures upon your heart. Confess and profess your love for the Lord every day. He abides with you as He desires to copilot your life's direction. But you must invite Jesus to take the wheel of your soul's destination, which is the extension of your surrendered heart. *Jesus, may You always be the Lord of my life and the center of my world.* Journal your journey forward!

~~~~~~~~~~~

God of Salvation, I pray to remain under Your wing of protection, mercy, grace, peace, and love all the days of my life. Manifest Yourself, as You multiply Your goodness over me, forevermore. Let everything I do always magnify Your name and be for Your glory. Amen.

_____
_____
_____
_____
_____
_____
_____
_____
_____
_____
_____
_____
_____

AFTERWORD

*T*hank you for choosing this ninety-day pilgrimage to develop into a transformed agent of change to begin seizing your God-ordained plan and purpose. However, the journey doesn't halt here! Don't brake yet, but push your pedal to the metal to pursue your divine destination, God's holy plan for you, and the redeemed purpose for your life's ultimate quest. Continue seeking daily, pray unceasingly, while exercising kindness and patience with yourself, especially during the seasons of clogged intersections that are blocking your pathway. Keep forging forward and remember that redemption is before you, not behind you! Keep your eyes on Jesus, as He will guide you on the highway to His heart through the front window of inspiration!

Please feel free to share your journey with me at pastorsharonumc@gmail.com.

CPSIA information can be obtained
at www.ICGtesting.com
Printed in the USA
JSHW022221260321
12966JS00003B/7